"Judith Siegel has given us a book with the force of revelation. Using exciting new research findings on brain physiology, she connects the emotional self to the body in which it lives in a manner that is both readable and wonderfully engaging. *Stop Overreacting* is a real tour de force; a book that is impossible to put down."

> —Maggie Scarf, author of *Intimate Partners: Patterns
> in Love and Marriage* and *Secrets, Lies, Betrayals:
> The Body/Mind Connection*

"Judith Siegel's *Stop Overreacting* captures the essential emotional problems that cause people distress. Even better, she clearly delineates very useful and accessible strategies for resisting emotional overload and destructive responses to emotional situations. *Stop Overreacting* is a valuable guidebook for navigating the basic struggles of our emotional world."

> —Beth Jacobs, Ph.D., clinical psychologist, adjunct faculty
> member of Northwestern University's Feinberg School of
> Medicine, and author of *Writing for Emotional Balance*

stop
overreacting

Effective
Strategies for
Calming Your
Emotions

JUDITH P. SIEGEL, PH.D., LCSW

New Harbinger Publications, Inc.

Publisher's Note

This publication is designed to provide accurate and authoritative information in regard to the subject matter covered. It is sold with the understanding that the publisher is not engaged in rendering psychological, financial, legal, or other professional services. If expert assistance or counseling is needed, the services of a competent professional should be sought.

Distributed in Canada by Raincoast Books

Copyright © 2010 by Judith P. Siegel
New Harbinger Publications, Inc.
5674 Shattuck Avenue
Oakland, CA 94609
www.newharbinger.com

FSC

Mixed Sources
Product group from well-managed
forests and other controlled sources

Cert no. SW-COC-002283
www.fsc.org
© 1996 Forest Stewardship Council

Acquired by Melissa Kirk; Cover design by Amy Shoup;
Edited by Elisabeth Beller; Text design by Tracy Marie Carlson

Library of Congress Cataloging-in-Publication Data

Siegel, Judith P.
  Stop overreacting : effective strategies for calming your emotions / Judith P. Siegel.
      p. cm.
  Includes bibliographical references.
  ISBN 978-1-57224-723-9
  1. Emotions. I. Title.
  BF531.S565 2010
  152'.4--dc22

                          2010011986

12   11   10

10 9 8 7 6 5 4 3 2 1   First printing

To Mitchell and Jenna—the next generation of writers

Contents

SECTION 1
The Mechanics

SECTION 2
The Triggers

SECTION 3
The Context

SECTION 4
New Strategies

Acknowledgments

Although many years have passed since I worked at Toronto's Hospital for Sick Children, my interest in neurobiology was sparked by the neurologists and patients I was privileged to work with there. I am deeply indebted to Dr. Gordon Murphy, Dr. Keith Meloff, and, above all, Dr. John Stobo Prichard, who opened my eyes to the mysteries of the brain. Shirley Stinson, who chaired the Social Work Department, was my supervisor and mentor and taught me how to translate book learning into competent clinical practice. The families I have worked with in Canada and in the United States have been my best instructors, and I am grateful to have had the opportunity to learn through my work with them.

I would also like to acknowledge my colleagues at the Silver School of Social Work at New York University. Special thanks go to Ann Marie Mareno, whose skill and commitment made it easier for me to concentrate on my writing projects.

Thanks are also due to my editors at New Harbinger, whose push for clarity improved this manuscript considerably. Melissa Kirk and Jess Beebe encouraged me to develop exercises that could help people acquire the kind of insight that is usually only possible in a therapy environment. The level of self-help that they envision for New Harbinger readers is inspiring. I offer my most sincere thanks to my copy editor, Elisabeth

Beller, who went beyond my expectations in order to help organize and complete the manuscript. Thanks also go to proofreader Jasmine Star.

I would also like to acknowledge family members who have supported this project from its inception. My sisters Shelley Fingerhut and Wendy Sokolowski Pezim and mother, Lillian Siegel, are always there for me when I need them. I am particularly grateful to my sister Debbie Naftolin, who has frequently helped me regain my own emotional equilibrium and who provided useful suggestions to improve and even name this book.

But above all, I would like to acknowledge two amazing teenagers who have pitched in and helped with Danny so that this book could be completed on time.

Introduction

Although we live in a complex world filled with challenges and disappointments, some people are better equipped to handle it than others. Why is it that some can reflect and respond to stressful situations in an honest but calm way while others just explode? Why do some withdraw or get deeply pessimistic when others can just let a troubling comment go? Have there been times when you found yourself so angry that you couldn't see straight? Do people ever tell you that your interpretation of events is way out of line? Have reactions that seemed justified at the time proven to be inappropriate and damaging? This book is written for people who realize that their behavior is often influenced by emotional turbulence that they don't understand and can't seem to control.

For years I have worked with people who have suffered the consequences of intense reactions. Only in hindsight can they reevaluate the actions that have hurt the people they love and complicated their lives. Perhaps this is your story as well. Perhaps you have lost your temper or made a hasty decision that has haunted you for years. If looking back on the things you have done in the past fills you with regret, then the information in this book may help you turn things around.

My approach to this problem is based on years of experience, as well as the latest research. In 1990, President George Bush announced financial support for research on neurobiology and started what is now dubbed the Decade of the Brain. This research confirmed the mind-body connection and has spawned hundreds of additional research studies that explain how the brain regulates emotions. Much of this research confirms my clinical experience with individuals, couples, and families who have struggled with problems that are created or exacerbated by emotional overreactions.

I view overreaction as an experience that involves both mind and body, past and present. In the first section of this book, I explain how beliefs, emotions, and physiological responses combine to create overreactions. In the second section, I examine envy, rejection, criticism, and control—everyday dynamics that frequently trigger overreactions. These chapters illustrate how an overreaction begins and unfolds, as well as ways to keep a more balanced perspective. In the third section, I present common situations that may arise in work and family relationships. Whether with coworkers, supervisors, customers, employees, spouses, parents, or children, overreactions can create havoc and complicate our lives. In the final section of this book, I review different strategies that will help you restore calm so that you can access responses that are thoughtful and appropriate. I also suggest ways to challenge beliefs and make peace with the past so that you will be less likely to react to situations that have triggered overreactions in the past.

To truly benefit from this book, you need to take three risks. The first risk involves doing the end-of-chapter exercises. After years of avoiding certain feelings and memories, you will be asked to spend time with them. This takes courage and trust but will provide you with new ways of understanding and coping with your emotional world. The second risk involves persistence. If you were overweight and out of shape, the thought of reading one book and then running a mile in nine minutes would sound great. But you probably know that it would take time to build up your stamina and that it might take a few days before you can even walk an entire mile. Learning to work with intense emotional responses is not that different. By learning to explore your emotional world in small segments, you will find that you build your capacity to tolerate emotions that have the potential to overwhelm you if they're not broken into smaller pieces. Each time you find a strategy that seems to help, you will need to practice it to achieve the end result you are seeking. The final risk involves self-acceptance. In this book I invite you to think about your life in new ways and with a new level of honesty.

As a therapist, I know that this process is much easier when you are able to share your feelings and insights with a professional who can offer encouragement and support. I hope that the discoveries you make on your own will be a sufficiently meaningful incentive to keep you moving closer to managing your reactions in a thoughtful way.

Throughout this book, I draw on case examples and composites of people I have seen in treatment over the past thirty years. It is my hope that you may see yourself in the stories of others who have experienced and overcome the destructive force of overreaction.

SECTION 1

The Mechanics

While it is tempting to hope that we could just learn a few tricks to help us stop overreacting, the best way to create long-lasting change begins with an understanding of the process. This section of the book will help define and clarify the different aspects of overreactions.

CHAPTER 1

Understanding Overreactions

Our reactions are created in a split second but may lead to actions that can reverberate for years. Although most of us would like to believe that our responses are justified and based on the truth, quite often this is simply not the case. Too often, a situation triggers old beliefs, expectations, and emotional memories that seep into the moment and color the way we interpret events. When this happens, our thoughts and feelings are no longer firmly rooted in the present. Even when we have no conscious awareness of these unfolding dynamics, our thoughts, feelings, and actions usually lead us to do something we later regret.

Before reading this book, you might have thought that overreacting meant having an emotional meltdown. Perhaps you remembered a time that you just lost it and exploded in an eruption of rage. But it is also possible to overreact in the opposite way and withdraw. Perhaps there was a time when something minor led to days of misery when you felt depressed and pessimistic. *Overreactions* are best understood as intense responses that are fueled by past experiences and raw emotions that have not been thoughtfully sorted out. In other words, our reaction takes place before we have registered and fully comprehended the specific factors that are producing our response. Sometimes our emotions are so intense, it is difficult to think at all. Other times our discomfort leads us to try to stop thinking about the situation entirely, even though it is almost impossible to escape from the feelings.

I have worked with clients who describe their moments of overreacting as "flicking a switch." Their thoughts and emotions seem to come out of nowhere and completely take over the moment. Other clients complain of ruminations or invasive thoughts and worries that they just can't shake. I completely understand what they are describing because I have had episodes of overreacting in my own life as well. If we are honest, all of us will acknowledge times when emotions took over and caused us to act in ways we later regretted. Knee-jerk reactions are part of the human experience, but some people are better able to identify their impulse to respond quickly and can use tools to help themselves regain a thoughtful perspective before any harm is done.

Identifying the issues that we tend to react to most strongly is part of knowing how to subdue overreaction. Frequently we have been exposed to something that makes us feel hurt or anxious. In this book, I will refer to that event as the *trigger* of the overreaction. Each of us has specific areas of sensitivity that we have pushed into the back of our awareness. Perhaps there were times in our childhoods that we felt threatened, diminished, shamed, or rejected. If the surge of emotional memory is too much for us to handle, our defenses step in to manage it for us. This chapter will examine the different kinds of responses and dynamics that occur when we overreact.

Not Everyone Reacts the Same Way

In the same way that we experience different degrees of hunger or sleepiness, we have a range of depth and intensity in our feeling world as well. When it comes to emotions, each one of us has a different comfort zone—both experiencing our own emotions and being stimulated by someone else's. Maybe you grew up in a family that was comfortable with open expressions of anger as well as affection. Family members might scream at each other for a few minutes and then end up laughing and hugging. Other families tend to disapprove of emotional displays and are reserved in how they show what they feel.

Each of us also has a different range of *emotional equilibrium*, or the degree to which we can manage stressful experiences in a calm and thoughtful way. Our emotional equilibrium is composed of many factors, including our temperaments, past experiences, and general states of well-being. Just as a young child is likely to have a temper tantrum when he is tired and hungry, we adults are more easily irritated and prone to overreaction when we are under physical or emotional stress. Lack of sleep also changes our brain chemistry in ways that prime us to overreact (Walker and van der Helm 2009). But even on the best day, each of us has a breaking point where the combined strength of the emotion that has been evoked and the emotional memories that have been stimulated is simply too much to bear.

The Exploder and the Imploder

Just as we each have our own personal breaking point, we all have different ways of showing it. While one person might not be able to contain her emotions and will just let it all out, someone else might react to feeling overwhelmed by becoming withdrawn and distant. These are equally powerful but fundamentally different responses. If you are the kind of person who tends to get agitated and loud, then you are an *exploder*. If you find yourself putting your feelings aside and trying to push upsetting things out of your mind, then you fall into the *imploder* category.

These two basic approaches to managing states of being overwhelmed tend to develop over time. There are hundreds of research studies that look at the different ways children react to stressful situations. Perhaps you can remember how you handled stress when you were in grade school. If you were one of the kids who acted up in class or on the playground, then you probably showed signs of being an exploder. Exploders have a difficult time holding their feelings in and easily become agitated and even aggressive when they are on overload. But children who internalize stress are having an equally difficult time. If you were the kind of child who imploded, your problems may not have been noticed by teachers and parents. People might have described you as being shy when you were actually too confused or overwhelmed to fully engage in what was going on. Kids who implode often escape notice until they show signs of being depressed or become physically ill with headaches or stomach cramps. Even then, adults don't always understand that children's symptoms may be related to holding their feelings in.

Why We React the Way We Do

When it comes to understanding patterns of behavior, there is usually a mix of nature and nurture at work. The way that you learned to manage your emotional reactions is a combination of things you inherited, such as temperament and genetic predisposition, as well as things that you were exposed to (Ochsner and Gross 2007). How your parents reacted to stress and problems is definitely one clue, but how they responded to you is equally telling. The messages that you picked up about showing emotions, and the value placed on being expressive versus being contained, are all contributing factors. Understanding your own unique style is an important part of learning to change it. Whether you cry, rage, withdraw, or become deeply pessimistic, there are probably better ways to cope with difficult moments.

Not All Strong Feelings Are Overreactions

Having a powerful feeling is not always a sign that you are overreacting. There is a depth and richness to life that comes from being able to connect to the feeling world. Under certain circumstances, strong emotions are entirely appropriate and even helpful. Often our feelings are signals of problems that need to be dealt with. Trying to build a buffer to dampen emotional awareness usually works against us and deprives us of enjoying moments of happiness. It is far better to commit to living an emotionally rich life that allows us to feel fully engaged. But there are times when we are strongly moved for reasons that we don't fully understand and that are inappropriate to the situation.

Sorrow, for example, is a feeling that we would expect if we suffer an important loss. But some of us tend to blow minor things out of proportion and experience an intensity that would only be called for if, indeed, the event was a true catastrophe. A parent who loses a child has faced a horrific experience that would normally be accompanied by extreme grief, sorrow, sadness, and anger. Having your team lose an important game is hardly tragic. Yet some people get thrown into a major funk or become enraged when their team doesn't make it through the playoffs.

To truly understand the difference between an appropriate feeling and an emotional overreaction, it is necessary to consider the steps that take place in our minds and bodies as we make connections between thinking and feeling. Some of us make rapid assessments and are suddenly overcome by extreme emotions. An exploder will just let it out and take a strong stance without making sure that his perceptions are accurate. An imploder will find the emotions that have been stimulated to be unbearable and will shut down as if the worst possibility has actually happened. In an overreaction, something about the situation has stimulated intense emotions, which are guided through a narrow interpretation and emerge as a rapid and poorly thought-out response.

In the next chapter, I will help you understand the important difference between intense emotions and intense feelings. Although you may not be aware of it, different parts of the brain work together to help us make sense of the world around us. When the thinking and feeling parts are working in harmony, we can use all of the information in a thoughtful way. However, some situations stimulate a knee-jerk emotional response that is caused by a neurological short circuit. At that moment, the thinking and emotional parts of our brain are disconnected, and we are unable to access all of our memories and working knowledge. I call these kinds of reactions *unprocessed*, as they are "raw" and emerge without reflection or self-awareness.

Unprocessed emotions are well-known to all of us, as they originate in childhood when we have fewer coping mechanisms. Usually just experiencing this emotional intensity creates anxiety, which complicates and exacerbates the experience. Even if we've learned more appropriate responses to certain emotions, the logical part of our brain isn't available to help us at that moment.

The answer to identifying overreaction has more to do with the process of the experience than with the intensity of the experience. There may be a straight line between the trigger and the response, but the one thing that has been left out is the most important aspect—thoughtful reflection.

Three Ingredients of Overreactions

All overreactions contain three ingredients: the event that triggers a sense of danger, an immediate response that involves our emotions as well as our physical state, and an interpretation of unfolding events that may be colored by defenses and emotional memories. Although researchers around the world debate the exact sequence and contribution of each aspect (Lewis 2005b), all agree that these components influence each other almost simultaneously. The way we view a situation has a profound effect upon our physical and emotional response; but our physical and psychological well-being at that point in time, as well as our acquired beliefs, also have a profound effect upon the way we view a situation. In the past decade, hundreds of published research studies have shed light on the different components that are involved in attaching factual and emotional meaning to events. The way that people comprehend and regulate their emotional responses has also become an important topic to psychotherapists from many different backgrounds. All of this new information about emotional regulation has led to cutting-edge strategies that can help you understand and change overreactions.

Consequences of Overreacting

How often have you lost your temper and lashed out with words or physical aggression? How many times have you felt so overwhelmed that you froze or felt like you were going to faint? Have you ever had a reaction that led you to feel paralyzed by deep despair and hopelessness? If we don't take the time to calm down enough to approach situations in a more thoughtful way, our responses usually create additional problems. Emotional overreactions often cause us as much pain as they cause for the people around us. Problems may seem impossible to solve, and relationships may seem worthless. Miserable moments may spread into days before somehow something inside us shifts and we are released from the spell.

Whether your style is to explode, implode, or do a little of both, there are always consequences. Feelings provide us with information that is vital to our well-being. Each time we become aware of a problem in our life, we have an opportunity to solve it. By understanding our feelings, we can learn a great deal about ourselves and the other people involved in any given situation. In contrast, a reaction that excludes thoughtful awareness makes it impossible to use the information that we could otherwise have learned from. By succumbing to our overreaction, we suffer the worst part of the event but compromise our ability to take hold of the feature that might actually be useful. We end up repeating rather then learning from our experience.

In each of the following examples, you'll meet people who experience an emotional response with little awareness of what's happening. They respond in different ways but are all filled with remorse later. The ways that they attempt to appease their guilt only reinforce the patterns that led them to be overwhelmed in the first place.

■ PAULA'S STORY

Paula was dismayed when she read her latest bank statement. On the one hand, she knew that she had been using her debit card a lot lately, but she had made a real effort to cut down on spending as much as she could. Instead of enjoying her morning cappuccino at the gourmet coffee house near her office, she was buying coffee from the office vending machine. She had replaced her expensive face cream with one from the drugstore and taken two pairs of shoes to be repaired so she wouldn't need to replace them. When her daughter, Carla, casually told her that she needed $80 to contribute to the limo for junior prom and that she had seen a cool dress for only $200, Paula snapped. She screamed at Carla that $200 was a great deal of money and that if $200 was not that big a deal, she should pay for it herself.

■ ANDY'S STORY

Andy had three files to clean up and at least twenty phone calls to return. Business had been tough recently. Just yesterday, the project he had been pitching for the past month had been rejected. When he tried to think about what he could have done differently to win the deal, he found himself second-guessing his pricing and doubting that he would have been able to do the work. The sight of the unanswered messages on his phone was too much to take. Wishing he could just take the rest of the week off, he sighed and looked at his computer screen. Then, glancing at the phone by his left hand and the bulging folders beside the mouse pad, he clicked on his solitaire game and just zoned out for the rest of the morning.

Consequences

Paula and Andy had little awareness of the triggers that caused them to overreact. After she exploded at her daughter, Paula was filled with remorse. Carla had been so helpful to her this past year, and Paula had fully intended to make her prom a special reward. Paula had always resented the fact that her own parents were absorbed by the special needs of her hyperactive younger brother and had little energy left over for her. They seemed to take her good behavior and excellent grades for granted and were stingy with presents or praise. From the time she entered high school, Paula had worked hard to be able to supply herself with small things that helped make her feel special. After Carla was born, she vowed that she would always do her best to make her daughter know how much she was valued. Paula juggled all her responsibilities in order to be an available and supportive parent and had done her best to reward Carla with the kinds of treats she had yearned for when she was a teenager. If her daughter now took those things for granted, then the fault was Paula's own.

After she snapped at her daughter, Paula was flooded with guilt. In the middle of offering an apology, she impulsively offered to buy Carla a new pair of shoes so that the prom outfit would be perfect. Paula's attempts to appease her guilt in this manner would only lead to more financial pressure and ultimately force her to sacrifice the few luxuries in her own life that helped her ward off the unbearable feeling of being deprived.

In a similar way, Andy regretted that he had wasted precious time by zoning out while on his computer. He couldn't explain to himself why he hadn't been able to focus on the work that needed to be done that day and felt even more discouraged and overwhelmed when he left the office. Andy couldn't remember the last time he had felt this tired and disorganized. He was used to winning deals and getting complimented for his creative and dynamic presentations. These days, he felt old and passed over. He resisted giving in to his sense of defeat, as it made him feel too much like his father. His father had moved across the country after divorcing Andy's mother, and although he called occasionally, Andy rarely saw him. His father had drifted from job to job and eventually developed a chronic health problem that left him unemployed and almost destitute. By not allowing himself to process the fear of failure that had been stimulated after one day of disappointment, Andy had awakened a dread of incompetence. His coping method of escape only took him closer to realizing his worst fears.

After the Overreaction

Without awareness, the problems that cause us to overreact lead to cycles of overreaction, remorse, compensation, and renewed angst. If we become loaded with feelings of guilt and regret for overreacting, we make it even worse for ourselves. How different it might have been if Paula and Andy could have connected their first emotional responses with the triggering circumstances. If only they could have recognized their feeling states and figured out that old emotional memories were fueling discomfort. To do that, they would first need to develop skills to help them process emotions.

End-of-Chapter Exercise: Do You Know Your Style?

To manage your reactions, it is important to begin by learning what kind of style you have. In this section, I'll help you become more aware of the way you tend to react. Consider the following questions:

- When someone gets very angry at you, do you tend to withdraw?

- Would people who know you describe you as someone who is mainly logical?

- When the stress in your life builds up, are you likely to feel fatigued or ill?

- When someone asks you how you are feeling, do you give them information about events instead of a description of your emotional experience?

- Do you often zone out or have escape fantasies?

If you said yes to most of these questions, then chances are that you fall into the imploder style.

Now think about these questions:

- Do you frequently lose your temper or fight about an issue that seems important in the moment but that you barely remember a few weeks later?

- Do you speak your mind if you think someone has acted inappropriately?

- When someone challenges you, do you get annoyed and stand up to them?

- When another car cuts you off in traffic, do you try to catch up to them or start swearing?

- Do people tell you that you are too emotional?

If you answered yes to most of these questions, then you probably are an exploder.

I don't know anyone who is always calm and fully aware of the things that might be troubling her at any given moment. But if you unleash your emotions before you can digest them, or if you avoid them in ways that preclude understanding, you may find yourself handling situations in ways you later regret.

CHAPTER 2

Processing Emotions

The past decade has produced extensive research on how the brain works. For years, mental health professionals have puzzled over the question of nature versus nurture in the study of personality and coping styles. Today, we have a clearer understanding of the ways in which heredity and upbringing influence the way you handle your emotions (Cozolino 2002; Kandel 1998, 1999). To learn how to get a handle on your responses, you should take the time to understand what is going on inside your brain that leads you to overreact.

How the Brain Operates

With the help of sophisticated research equipment, social scientists and neuroscientists have a much better understanding of how different parts of the brain contribute to the processing of emotions (Lewis 2005a; Phelps and LeDoux 2005). If you were in a lab during an outburst or a shutdown, the technician could show you brain images that reveal exactly what is going on in your brain before and during your overreaction. You would be able to see the parts of your brain that are activated and, of equal importance, the *neural pathways* (or *circuits*) that connect the different parts of your brain. While a brain scan might look like a piece of art to your untrained eye, these technological advances have created a major shift in the way therapists understand emotional disorders.

Left Brain and Right Brain

Dr. Alan Schore (2003a), a leader in this field, has summarized the different parts of the brain that are responsible for feeling and thinking. The left brain is primarily responsible for the thinking skills we need. The right brain, especially the right frontal system, houses emotional states and affective experiences. Many episodes of overreaction are created when the amygdala, located in the right brain, is overstimulated (Rauch, Shin, and Wright 2003). When the amygdala is activated, it sets off a chain of events. Most important is the production of noradrenaline and neurohormones that contribute to a state of heightened arousal. This happens in a split second, and you may not even notice the changes in your body that this creates.

In this state of heightened arousal, you are stimulated to respond in ways that have been genetically hardwired into the human species. Drs. Rick Hanson and Richard Mendius (2009) explain that we process information in different parts of the brain. The amygdala primes our bodies to rev up so that all of our available energy can help us fight or run away if we need to. Many parts of the brain then work together to glean information that will help us determine the best plan of action. However, this requires that the different parts of the brain be able to communicate quickly and efficiently to help quiet things down if all that extra energy isn't needed. Unfortunately, it takes longer for the brain to access acquired knowledge in order to make the best decision possible, and the pathways that coordinate acquired wisdom with perceived danger cannot always interact in a way that works toward thoughtful appraisal (LaBar and Cabeza 2006). Under certain circumstances, the parts of the left brain that regulate higher levels of reasoning are bypassed. When this happens, we are primed to fight or flee but are unable to draw on the information that would help us reach the most useful conclusions.

Thinking and Feeling

By studying how different people respond to similar traumas, psychiatrists have recognized the importance of the neural circuitry and, in particular, the connections between the left and right parts of the brain. One of the most important differences between people who cope reasonably well and those who overreact is the ability to connect thoughts and feelings. The stronger the circuits that connect left and right, the better able you are to tolerate and diffuse intense emotions (D. J. Siegel 1999).

Dr. John Gottman (1998) studied couples in conflict and demonstrated the difficulty of integrating rational thought when the amygdala is firing. Spouses who had been identified as having highly conflictual marriages were easily provoked into fighting with each other. They quickly became angry and tended to dismiss or reject each other's views. Not surprisingly, laboratory tests done during their arguments confirmed high levels of corticosteroids that indicated amygdala involvement. After their arguments were interrupted and they'd had time to calm down, their stress hormones and other physical markers returned to normal levels. Only then could each truly understand what the other had been trying to say during the argument. In a state of high arousal, people just can't attend to new information or communicate in a thoughtful way.

If the right brain takes the lead when we become stressed, our ability to comprehend potentially important information is compromised (Gohm 2003). As arousal and anxiety subside, we are better able to register and integrate ideas that just couldn't be processed earlier. Usually this information allows us to rethink some of the rapid assumptions we have made and revise our conclusions. The stronger the connections between the left and right brain, the better able we are to stay with an emotional experience, reflect on it, and ultimately respond in ways that are productive for everyone involved.

Emotions or Feelings

Sophisticated brain-imaging technology has also helped researchers understand the neurological differences between emotions and feelings.

Dr. Mona Fishbane (2007) stresses the difference between the two. *Emotions* occur in the right brain regardless of a person's age, ethnicity, or education. These basic emotions include happiness, sadness, anger, disgust, and fear. In contrast, *feelings* are produced when the thinking (left) and emotional (right) parts of the brain work together to achieve an understanding of the emotional experience. Strong neural pathways between the left and right brain help us become more aware of our own feeling world as well as the feelings of others (Schore 2003b; D. J. Siegel 2003).

Anger, for example, is an emotion that might be produced in a variety of situations. You might be angry if your children refuse to listen to you, your boss asks you to work late at the very last minute, a car cuts you off in traffic, or you get home after a twenty-minute drive and realize that the cashier at the restaurant gave you someone else's take-out order. The *emotion* is anger, but the *feelings* in each situation might be completely different. When your children disregard your authority, you might feel resentful that you now need to become the bad guy and enforce a punishment. If your own parents were overly strict and you had vowed to be more of a friend than an authority, your resentment would be even more profound. If your boss asks you to work late, you might begin to feel helpless or envious of a coworker who left early and wasn't around to share the job. When someone cuts you off in traffic, you might feel diminished, as if you are insignificant or unimportant. It might remind you of times when people assumed that you wouldn't stand up for yourself and took away things you were entitled to. Opening up the wrong dinner order might make you feel furious at the cashier's incompetence. You might find that your standards for your performance, as well as that of others, are extremely high and that you cannot tolerate people who make stupid mistakes. On the surface, these situations create the emotion of anger; below the surface, they create feelings of resentment, envy, worthlessness, and lack of control.

Self-Awareness

When it comes to self-awareness, there is a wide spectrum of ability. At one end, there are people who seem to have easy access to a full range of responses. They can identify dozens of different feeling states and can even sort through a combination of different feelings that are operating at the same time. At the other end of the scale, there are people who seem completely cut off from feeling-state awareness and instead only register the facts. They may have intense emotional reactions, but they have little or no ability to describe or even focus on the way that they feel before or during the event. They can tell you what they think but not what they feel.

Once again, the connections between different parts of the brain seem to make all the difference. Researchers have identified the brain processes that help us connect emotional reactions with working memory and language (Viamontes and Beitman 2006). Other researchers have examined the neural circuits that connect the parts of the brain that generate emotion-based impulses with the parts that store the working memory we rely on to make sound decisions (LaBar and Cabeza 2006). Without the ability to think about how our emotional responses will impact our future, our judgment is simply not there to guide us.

Many rash actions that we deeply regret are created when impulses generated in the amygdala can not be processed by particular parts of our brains. However, it is possible to strengthen the necessary connections so that recognizing, naming, and weighing consequences can work together more smoothly.

■ DYLAN'S STORY

Dylan liked to think of himself as a happy-go-lucky kind of guy. In fact, most of his friends would describe him that way. He was the first one to tell a joke and had a knack for making other people laugh. When his friends complained about work or minor health problems, Dylan would know exactly what to say to help them find the humorous side and shift their mood. The two exceptions to this were golf and parenting. Dylan was an excellent golfer and usually went through the round with a grin on his face. But if he flubbed a shot or couldn't get out of a sand trap, he would curse in a loud voice that made everyone uncomfortable. If he had a few bad shots in a row, he would throw his club, and once he even threw his whole golf bag into a creek. This temper problem was even worse at home. If the kids didn't listen to him, he would shout in a very loud voice and threaten to take away all of their privileges. He started therapy after he took a swing at his ten-year-old son. Fortunately, his son ducked the blow, but he might have been seriously injured if his father's fist had connected. Dylan's wife said that if he didn't start therapy immediately, she would call the police and Child Protective Services.

In therapy, Dylan said that he just didn't know what had come over him. He claimed that he was perfectly calm one minute and then would feel so enraged that he would start to shake. His face would turn red, and he would do whatever came to his mind. Dylan was surprised to hear that he could learn to measure anger by paying attention to different parts of his body and that, even if his rage mounted quickly, he could notice how his stomach, neck, and throat felt when the anger first started. Dylan was also curious about my observation that he seemed particularly reactive to situations where he was made to feel incompetent. His son's defiance had made him feel that he had no control over his child's behavior and that his son was going to walk all over him. Feeling diminished and incapable of getting it right were important triggers that unleashed powerful childhood memories.

Although Dylan started from the position that he had no control over or explanation for his anger or why he just lost it, he had plenty of memories of running away from his dad, who was also prone to episodes of rage. When Dylan was able to understand how sensitive memories could cause his interpretation of events to be magnified, he was able to learn to warn himself when he started to feel powerless or diminished. That, combined with his ability to recognize anger when it started, helped him learn to remove himself from the situation until he could regain his calm, separate his current experience from the emotional memories that were causing him to overreact, and use his better judgment.

Processing Emotions

Perhaps you, like many others, have been trying to learn ways to understand and manage your feelings. Getting information from books and articles is definitely a first step, but reading by itself seldom yields immediate results. Why? Like other things that are stored in our memory bank, that vital information simply may be bypassed once the amygdala takes over. Research suggests that information is processed and retained in a part of the brain that may not be available at the moment when intense emotions are triggered (Cyders and Smith 2008; Ochsner and Gross 2007). Even if you have acquired new information that *could* be useful to you, you won't have access to it during an overreaction unless you can calm yourself enough to access it. During peak emotional experiences, self-awareness is possible only when the circuits in the brain allow the emotional and logical parts to inform each other.

Parents' Roles in Creating Neural Pathways

It probably won't surprise you to learn that therapists are very interested in researching the processes that help create optimal neural pathways. The way that parents respond to their children's emotional distress seems particularly important. Level of security is another key ingredient that helps children cultivate pathways between the thinking and feeling parts of the brain (Cicchetti and Tucker 1994; deZulueta 2006). Children who are soothed by responsive parents and given the kind of consistent home life that allows them to trust their caretakers are better prepared to cope with potentially distressing situations than children who are ignored or criticized when they need comforting.

Children whose parents help them to regain their calm have a distinct advantage over children whose parents become overly anxious and worried themselves. Children's feelings of being protected and joined in the process of resolving a problem help create a sense of trust and safety. The ideal parenting response allows children to talk about problems and share feelings without being rebuffed or overwhelmed by their parents' response. Parents who become agitated or take on their children's anxieties are only adding to their children's belief that feelings are dangerous. Rather than absorb a child's emotional state, parents need to soothe the child and then help the child sort out feelings, fears, and possible solutions (D. J. Siegel and Hartzell 2003).

■ BRENDA'S STORY

When I started to work with Brenda, I was concerned about her health. In the previous year she had suffered from several infections, severe headaches, and a back spasm that had confined her to bed for a week. She was very thin and told me that she frequently suffered from gastrointestinal distress and irritable bowel syndrome. As the mother of two preschool children and a ten-year-old with Tourette syndrome, she was under a lot of stress. I quickly learned that there were financial and marital problems as well. Brenda had quite a few friends she could choose to talk with, but often she kept her feelings to herself.

I asked Brenda to tell me about her parents and whether they had been interested in helping her handle her stress when she was younger. It turned out that Brenda's mother had been too interested in trying to help her daughter. If Brenda started to talk to her mother about being chastised by a teacher or excluded from a friend's party, her mother would react to the situation as if she had been unfairly reprimanded or left out. Rather than respond to her daughter's feelings, her mother would get upset and start to swear and threaten to do all kinds of rash things that frightened Brenda. Her mother's agitation could last for hours, until the positions were reversed and Brenda ended up trying to calm down her mother. These kinds of experiences taught Brenda that it was more burdensome to unload her feelings than to keep them private. The cost of having to take care of her mother and her fear that her feelings could lead to more serious problems convinced her to keep her feelings to herself.

Shutdown

Genetic predisposition, temperament, and situational factors all contribute to the level of distress a child experiences. But a child who is in a state of agitation or protest and can't be soothed will only remain in a state of acute distress for so long. Sooner or later, the level of emotional intensity escalates to an unbearable physiological tension that leads her to shut down (Krystal 1988; van der Kolk, McFarlane, and Weisaeth

1996). The process of numbing the self or completely tuning out the stress is basically a strategy for immediate psychological survival, but one that creates neural circuitry that works against the integration of thoughts and feelings.

■ NANCY'S STORY

Nancy was the youngest child born to parents who were miserable in their marriage. By the time Nancy was born, her parents slept in separate bedrooms, and her mother was bitter that her life was confined to a husband she no longer respected and to children who seemed unappreciative of what she had to offer them. For most of her childhood, Nancy was on her own, getting little solace or comfort from her self-absorbed parents. She learned to take care of herself and to focus on the things she could control.

Nancy excelled at school and sports and had a small group of friends who had similar interests. She preferred to keep busy and had little patience for people who wallowed in self-pity. She rarely asked for help and was proud of her self-sufficiency. Things almost fell apart for her the day after she accepted her boyfriend's marriage proposal. In an effort to clear the air, he had confessed to her that despite an earlier promise to be sexually exclusive, he had remained sexually involved with a former girlfriend. Nancy was momentarily overpowered by dizziness, but she said nothing. When the room stopped spinning, she decided to call her closest girlfriend. As her friend listened to Nancy's factual description, she expressed amazement that Nancy wasn't furious or in tears. Nancy's logical approach to the situation seemed cold and calculating and was completely devoid of feelings.

When her friend asked how she was feeling, Nancy answered in her typically calm and collected way that her read on the situation was that she should go ahead with the wedding plans. She focused on the fact that because he had chosen to confide his infidelity, nothing was seriously wrong. For the next few months, Nancy found that by keeping extra busy, she could prevent those momentary twinges of doubt and stay optimistic that the future would be just fine.

Nancy is an imploder: she represses her emotions rather than lashing out with them. When she first learned about her boyfriend's infidelity, she was flooded with anxiety. However, rather than understand her reaction of becoming light-headed as a signal of strong emotions, she shut down entirely from her feeling world. When her friend asked her how she was feeling, she simply stated the facts as she saw them. Because there was no place in her learned experience from childhood for self-pity or self-doubt, she repackaged the information in a way that allowed her to feel secure and in control. Later she would come to see how she had glossed over information that should have been more thoughtfully processed. Shutting down leads to an illusion that things are under control, but at a considerable expense. The numbing leads to a deadening of emotional life and prevents us from dealing with problems that need to be addressed. Although an implosion may look less disruptive than a meltdown, there is a similar rupture between thoughts and feelings that leaves us unable to fully process and respond to the situation.

Creating Options

Being able to process feelings is a key ingredient to knowing yourself and to empathizing or understanding someone else's feelings. Even if you didn't grow up in a family that was emotionally attuned, it is never too late for you to develop new neural pathways. Regardless of your age and childhood experiences, you have the potential to build new mechanisms for processing emotions. Every time you are able to talk about your emotional experience with someone who cares and consider an emotionally charged situation from multiple perspectives, you are developing new circuits between the left and right parts of your brain (D. J. Siegel 1999).

Important pathways can also be created by strengthening connections from top to bottom. Neuroscience research has shown that impulsive and scattered responses are generated by the lower areas of the brain (Cyders and Smith 2008). By asking ourselves about consequences and searching stored memory for lessons we may have learned, we activate the higher areas of the brain responsible for planning and executing complex strategies (Farmer 2009). The networks between left and right and top and bottom can be strengthened through practice. With this in mind, know that it is never too late to learn how to become more attuned and tolerant of feelings. Learning that this is possible is one of the most promising new developments of recent decades, and it can help you learn to understand and overcome overreactions.

Developing Emotional Awareness

We all have different emotional comfort zones. When a powerful emotion overcomes us, we may be so overwhelmed that our first response is to run away from the experience through numbing, shutting down, seeking distractions, or using anger to expel it. However, the process of identifying and naming the emotion can stimulate the left-brain–right-brain circuits and point us in the right direction.

Many psychologists have suggested that it is easier to work with feelings after you learn how to approach them. I have worked with many intelligent, successful people who have learned to survive through their skill at analyzing problems, but whose overreliance on thinking is accompanied by an underreliance on feeling. A rational stance that doesn't incorporate feelings won't make you happy or fulfilled and very often creates problems in relationships.

I explain to my clients that their years spent thinking about problems can be compared to developing expertise in hiking and navigating hilly terrain. Some have become accomplished mountain climbers and have acquired the boots, ropes, and ice axes that help them excel. But in this analogy, their feeling world is the water, and they must now learn to swim. Their mountaineering gear will not help them here—and will likely hold them back.

Learning to swim requires new skills and the confidence that you can learn to do it. Experiencing emotions might be uncomfortable, but the discomfort is short-lived and unlikely to cause any harm. If you were emotionally overwhelmed when you were a child, you might automatically become anxious when your emotions begin to stir. But by spending time learning to identify and explore your feeling world, you will become less uncomfortable and more curious when you find yourself becoming emotional.

To learn how to tolerate feelings, you will need to learn how to identify them. I have organized feeling states in ways that may help you dig a little deeper and stretch your awareness.

When you feel *angry*, you may also be feeling

afraid	aggravated
agitated	annoyed
appalled	betrayed
bitter	cranky
disappointed	disgusted
exasperated	frustrated
helpless	hostile
irritated	jealous
let down	nervous
offended	pessimistic
provoked	repulsed
riled	tense
vicious	

When you feel *happy*, you may also be feeling

accomplished	amused
charmed	cheerful
delighted	elated
enthusiastic	excited
glad	joyful
peppy	proud
validated	

When you are *content*, you may also be feeling

appreciative	calm
fortunate	reflective
relaxed	soothed

When you feel *hurt*, you may also be feeling

cheated	defeated
deprived	deserted
diminished	forgotten
insulted	isolated
lonely	neglected
persecuted	slighted
snubbed	upset

When you feel *inadequate*, you may also be feeling

diminished	helpless
incompetent	inferior
pessimistic	powerless
useless	

The first step in connecting brain circuits is to become attuned to your emotional world. When you read a word that represents a feeling, you are using your intellectual understanding and activating your left brain. To become comfortable with the feeling world, it is important to register the physical and emotional experience that occurs in your right brain so that you can comprehend what you are feeling in that moment. The process of knowing your feelings is such a fundamental and necessary part of learning to stop overreacting that several exercises are presented here to get you started.

Take a closer look at each word in the preceding lists of feelings. Ask yourself if you can remember a time when you experienced each feeling. Dr. Beth Jacobs (2004) suggests that starting a journal for writing exercises is a wonderful way to help you get acquainted with different feelings during times that you are relaxed. To expand awareness and tolerance, Dr. Jacobs recommends tackling each feeling, one at a time, in your journal or notebook. She suggests one exercise that is designed to help you understand that feelings occur in increments: Concentrate on one feeling and write about a time when you felt that way slightly. Then write about a time when you had a more intense experience with that feeling. Finally, write about a time when you felt that way very strongly. We sometimes need to remind ourselves that not all feelings occur in the extreme and that, even if they feel dangerous in the moment, we can tolerate them once we create a safe distance.

Another exercise Dr. Jacobs developed helps you become familiar with feelings by approaching them in a new way. When you are in an emotional neutral zone, choose one of the feelings that you want to understand better from the lists above. To increase awareness of how you experience that particular feeling, ask yourself the following questions: If it was a color, what would it be? If it was a landscape, what would it be? If it was a piece of music, what would it be? You may not realize it, but there is already a strong connection between your senses and your feeling world. The next time you are watching a scary movie or TV show, pay attention to the music that is used in the scenes that create the most suspense. Look more closely at the smells that are used in aromatherapy or bath products that make you feel relaxed or invigorated. Our senses and our feeling world can be mutually informative.

If you take the time to acquaint yourself with each of the feelings on the lists above, you will have accomplished an important first step toward learning how to swim in the ocean of your feeling world. When you lose your fear of the water, you will learn to relax and enjoy it instead of fighting to stay above it. Rather than struggle to keep your eyes focused on the mountaintop, which is more familiar, you will learn that there is beauty and wonder in the waters you have avoided for so long.

Developing Mind-Body Awareness

Many people are surprised to learn how intertwined our minds and bodies really are. Deep emotional responses are accompanied by stress hormones that can be experienced in different parts of the body. Our muscles, digestive tract, circulatory system, and central nervous system have different ways of "knowing" and reacting to different feelings. Sometimes, a change in the physical self is the first signal we have that an event is evoking an intense emotional response.

Ultimately, your goal is to learn to notice the subtle physical responses that occur as you experience different emotions. Emotional responses rarely emerge in full-blown intensity, even though it may seem that way. Usually, there are stirrings and physical changes that can alert you to an impending storm if you know how to read your radar map.

By focusing on the different physical sensations that accompany specific feelings, you are opening up a new world of information. Learning to recognize and describe feelings may sound easy, but it is actually quite challenging, as well as extremely important to your overall emotional well-being. All of this information will help you face difficult moments in an entirely new way—a way that allows you to prevent overreaction.

End-of-Chapter Exercises

Learning to navigate the world of feelings can be both scary and fascinating. These exercises are designed to help you become more familiar with feelings. Chances are, the more you practice, the more comfortable you will become.

Exercise 1: Body Scan

Scanning your body for information is an important skill that will help you identify emotional responses and feelings as they first arise. It is also another way of strengthening brain circuits as you learn to notice and make sense of the physical, thinking, and feeling components of your life.

Part 1

Start from a neutral, relaxed position in a setting where you have few distractions. You might want to close your eyes as you zero in on the different parts of your body.

Ask yourself if you are aware of carrying any tension in your body. Do any of your muscles feel tense or uncomfortable? How rapidly is your heart beating? Are you aware of any tightness in your neck or chest? Think about how your hands feel. Are your fingers clenched or open? Do your palms seem sweaty or dry? What does your gut feel like? Feelings occur in our bodies as well as our minds. When you know how your body is when you are relaxed, you will by able to notice how you change under stress or during an emotional upheaval.

Part 2

Go back to the lists of feelings earlier in this chapter. Choose one of the feelings that you want to learn more about. Try to remember an actual experience that made you feel this way. Spend a minute or two recovering as many details as you can until you begin to feel the emotion as if you were back in the experience. Now, do another body scan. Ask yourself all the questions posed in part 1 of this exercise: How does your body feel during this particular emotional state? Think about the tension you may be carrying in different parts of your body. If you are uncomfortable, where do you notice it the most? If you feel better, can you notice it in any part of your body? By noticing the different physical sensations that accompany specific feelings, you are opening up a new world of information.

Part 3

Now try a guided scan. Just as difficult situations can create unpleasant emotional and physical reactions, wonderful experiences are also registered in our bodies and feelings. When we revisit these experiences, our memories can re-create the mood and physical state that we experienced at that moment. In this exercise, I want you to think about a memory of a time when you felt very happy or very safe. The memory you select for this exercise might be from a time when you were on vacation or in the company of someone who loves you or has protected you. Think about what happened that pleased you the most. What do you see? What do you hear? Do you remember any particular smells? Try to go back in time so that the details of all of your senses can be recovered. You will find that after spending a few minutes thinking about the details of one specific memory, your body and mood will shift under the influence of this positive emotional memory. Do another body scan to notice the effect that this memory has on you.

If you have cut yourself off from your feeling world, then you have been deprived of the curative and restorative power of feelings. When we learn how to allow a positive experience to register in our minds and bodies, we are developing an antidote to the stress that accumulates, regardless of our ability to identify it. By learning to memorize a wonderful moment with all of your senses, you can create a storehouse of positive experiences to replenish you and help you get through a difficult time. If you open yourself up to positive feelings, such as joy, pride, gratitude, comfort, and affection, you will become more attuned to moments that have the power to add to your reservoir of well-being (Fosha 2000).

Exercise 2: Making Connections

Each time you are able to share an important experience with another person, you have the opportunity to enhance the connections between the left and right parts of your brain. This exercise requires a willing partner who understands the goal and is prepared to experiment with you. It is better to speak face-to-face, but the exercise can be done over the phone as well. If you can't think of anyone you could safely do this with right now, then consider my comments at the end of this exercise regarding the benefits of joining a group.

Part 1

You will now work with a partner to create empathy. Ask your partner to talk about something important that happened to her recently—something that doesn't directly relate to you or a shared friend or family member. As your partner describes the situation, try to picture what it must have been like for her. Think about how she was feeling at that moment. Try to put yourself in her position. When she has finished telling her story, try to identify one or two feelings she may have experienced. It is up to the two of you to decide if you should make comments to one another or just thank your partner for sharing something important.

Part 2

Now it's your turn to share. Tell your partner something that's happened to you recently that doesn't involve her directly. As you speak, try to identify the way you were feeling. When you are finished, your friend may comment on feelings she registered. Remember, your friend or partner is commenting on her own feeling response and may not have processed your story as you did. Some people are very skilled at mirroring back the feelings they have received; others find that something has triggered them to focus on their own memories and feelings. However, your partner is doing her best to understand your story and respond in an honest way. Even if she hasn't fully understood your experience, the most important part of this exercise is the opportunity for you to put your thoughts and feelings together in a conversation. If you are able to do that, then your partner's response is just the icing on the cake. If you did find that her response mirrored what you were saying, then acknowledge how helpful that has been.

Each time you pause to connect your ideas and feelings, you are opening up and strengthening the channels that connect different parts of your brain. When you do this in an atmosphere where you feel encouraged and supported, your comfort level with speaking about your feelings will grow automatically.

This exercise can also work in groups that have been designed to support people who are going through similar experiences. Consider the advantages of learning to explore the emotional realm with people who don't know you at work or in the ordinary parts of your day. Self-help groups exist for people who are experiencing relationship transitions, adjusting to new communities, acting as caretakers for family members who are ill, and more. People who have similar circumstances (such as managing medical conditions or raising children without a partner) often benefit from learning how others handle similar problems. There are also groups for people supporting each other in fighting addiction and other kinds of mental illnesses, such as depression or obsessive-compulsive disorder (OCD). If you have never before taken the risk to spend a few hours in a support group, this might be the perfect opportunity to take that chance. Allowing yourself to empathize with others and share your own feelings with those who understand what you are going through can help you shift your brain circuits to respond in new ways.

CHAPTER 3

Interpreting Events

Recall that there are three ingredients in an overreaction: the event that has triggered a sense of danger, an immediate response that involves our emotions as well as our physical state, and an interpretation of unfolding events that may be colored by defenses and emotional memories. The worlds of thoughts and feelings are not as distinct from each other as some people would like to believe. The brain tends to interpret events very quickly, using assumptions and expectations that are not always appropriate. While most of us could explain what we think about a number of issues, we do not always understand the unchallenged assumptions that have led us to those positions.

Are You Seeing Clearly?

To understand the power of tacit beliefs, I often use the analogy of lenses like the ones that are used in cameras or eyeglasses. Our beliefs add certain hues to the lenses through which we view the world. Sometimes the scene in front of us takes on a color that belongs more to the glasses than to the actual landscape. Our beliefs can also magnify or reduce the subject matter, leading us to believe that things are much closer or farther away than they actually are. When this happens, something we need to be taking notice of may fade into the background, while we end up overfocusing on something that is relatively unimportant. However, unlike sunglasses or a camera, the filters created by our beliefs slip into place silently, so that we may not even know they are in operation.

Beliefs about ourselves and the people we are tied to are closely linked to a memory system that contains past events along with the feelings that were experienced at the time of the event. Rapid response is a necessary part of life, and we rarely take time to question what memories or beliefs might be influencing the way we interpret a certain incident. In fact, our minds are constantly sorting through stored information to access pieces of acquired knowledge that will help us interpret given moments (Lewis and Todd 2007).

With the help of neuroimaging equipment, researchers are becoming more aware of the parts of the brain that we use to help us navigate relationships. Even though it may only take us a few seconds to react to a situation, several areas of the brain may be called upon. Situations that involve nonverbal behavior or inference are actually quite complex and depend on different parts of the brain than just the part that decodes language (Ochsner and Gross 2007). Our long-term memories are stored in yet another part of the brain and are often needed to help us make sense of the relationships we have at home and at work. The more connections that are required between different parts of the brain, the greater the potential for error (Compton 2003; Grawe 2006). Inevitably, we must focus on certain aspects and discount others.

Revived Beliefs

Problems arise when a situation triggers an intense emotion that we don't fully understand. When this happens, previous experiences that share the same emotional flavor as the current event are resurrected to help us quickly make sense of what is going on. Most of the time this works to our advantage, allowing us to use acquired wisdom. The problem occurs when the beliefs that have been stimulated do not truly apply to the present moment.

Beliefs and former experiences can infiltrate the present with tremendous force. Once we have found a memory that resonates with the emotions of the current experience, we are automatically guided to focus on the parts that are similar and to use our experience to predict what is most likely to happen next. As our working memory guides us to focus on the information that is likely to be most helpful to us, our brain may highlight certain aspects of a situation while obscuring others. Like the lenses in a pair of glasses, our beliefs have the potential to sharpen our understanding and add clarity. But beliefs that are not entirely pertinent to the present situation can distort what we are viewing, leading us to see things in ways that are skewed or blurred. Most of the time, we are not even aware that we are wearing lenses that can so drastically shape our understanding and interpretation of the world around us.

Schemas

The way people decipher and respond to the world around them is an area of extensive research. Dr. Aaron Beck (1976) and Dr. Mardi Horowitz (1991) have pioneered concepts that are useful for understanding this process. One of the most helpful of these concepts is schemas, which refers to the way that we attach meaning to events. *Schemas* are mental maps that store and organize information so that acquired knowledge can be used to interpret current events very quickly. For instance, most of us know that if we notice a red flashing light on the roof of the car behind us, we should pull over and speak respectfully if the police officer asks us to answer some questions.

Cognitive psychology also explores the ways that schemas based on past relationships play a role in the present (Benjamin and Friedrich 1991; Young, Klosko, and Weishaar 2003). You may not realize it in the moment, but your expectations of how you are likely to be treated or how a situation will unfold is influenced by things that happened to you many years ago. This is particularly true in intimate relationships, where the sense of family can easily evoke schemas that existed between parent and child. For example, if you were made to feel valued by your parents, you will expect to feel valued by intimate partners.

However, in order to completely understand the power of schemas, you must consider the emotions that were experienced in the events that were stored. If your parents emphasized the importance of studying and getting good grades in school, you may feel comfortable relating to others who have high expectations of you. However, that schema has the potential to evoke two different and conflicting expectations and feelings: If parents with high expectations praised you because you studied and did well on an exam, your schema concerning living up to expectations most likely would contain pride and a sense of accomplishment. However, if the exam wasn't as easy as you expected, a poor grade might lead to a very different schema. Failing to meet your parents' expectations would create a schema that contains intense feelings of shame and doubt about being good enough to ever please your parents. Both schemas involve situations where a child is judged by his parents, but the beliefs and emotional memories would be completely different. The child who is praised for doing well in school but rejected or disciplined for poor performance may feel proud of his intelligence but very sensitive to cues that he has failed to do his best. For him, being less than 100 percent successful may create intense feelings of shame or self-loathing.

Emotionally Laden Beliefs

How different schemas get activated is a subject of interest to many psychologists (Hedwig and Epstein 1998). Psychologists now believe that just as thinking about a memory can evoke emotions, having an emotional experience can evoke old memories (Grawe 2006). For example, if we notice that someone is staring at us in a very stern and disapproving manner, we might suddenly feel very uncomfortable in a way that is identical to an earlier experience when we were challenged by someone in authority. Even if we can't remember the name of a teacher whose scrutiny and disapproval provoked discomfort, the lessons learned from activated memories take over, leading us to believe that what happened before will happen again. From that point on, we focus on information that would only be useful to us in a repeat situation but might be irrelevant and possibly misleading in situations that are actually different. We automatically use the information stored in old schemas to guide us through the present moment and to help us predict what is likely to happen next. Although there are times that this can work in our favor, it can also work against us (Goldin et al. 2009).

■ WILLIAM'S STORY

William's mother was an efficient woman who managed a house-hold that included a husband who traveled frequently and their seven children, who were close in age. As a middle child, William had the benefit of having an older brother who had paved the way for some freedom at an early age but the mixed blessing of two older sisters who were just as domineering as their mother. Unlike his sisters, William was more interested in sports than school, and he resented being told when to study or go to bed. William learned that being home put him under the scrutiny of the women in his family. If he was home when his family discovered a failing exam grade or a poorly done chore, he would have to listen to endless criticism. Nothing he did seemed to meet their standards. However, if he managed to slip away, it seemed that everyone got busy or distracted with other things and he was off the hook.

William was not able to succeed in any job that required him to work in an office or directly with a supervisor. However, he landed a sales job that allowed him to manage different accounts in different locations and he made a good income. His most pressing problem was his marriage. The week before they started therapy, his wife had threatened to divorce him unless he changed. She accused him of not caring and not participating in their family life. Every time that she wanted to get him involved in handling the children or the family finances, he would agree to whatever she proposed but not follow through. From his point of view, if he didn't do exactly what she wanted when she wanted it, he was going to be criticized, so why even bother? He didn't understand why, but every time she had a plan that involved him, he was filled with dread. He loved his wife and children but needed to have plenty of commitments and projects outside of the home so that he had an excuse to leave the house when things got uncomfortable.

In William's schema, women with plans that included him were dangerous. His mother and sisters would scrutinize his performance and, quite frequently, impose limits on his freedom to teach him a lesson. The schema of having a woman place an expectation on him was accompanied by a fear that he wouldn't be able to perform and anticipation that he would have restrictions placed on him. Years later, any attempt his wife made to involve him in parenting or figuring out their finances filled him with the same sense of dread. The experience of being asked for something by a woman was all that was needed to conjure up the old schema of scrutiny and punishment. His assumption that his wife would do the same thing pushed him to agree and then to escape in order to avoid the consequences. Motivation to avoid something unpleasant is a driving force that can activate our thoughts, feelings, and behavior.

Identifying Stored Schemas

Whether the schema has been revived because of a certain feeling or something about the circumstance, once it is in place we view the present situation in a very restricted way. It is useful to know some of the schemas that tend to resurface in moments of tension, but it is impossible to know all of the possible belief systems that can lead you to overreact. However, there are themes that tend to be repeated in the way we interact with others. Often, experiences from childhood continue to inform the way we interpret and respond to situations in our adult lives. If you are able to identify the beliefs and expectations that resurface when you overreact, you may be better able to notice when problematic schemas have resurfaced. As you will see in chapter 12, there are ways to recognize and eliminate the lenses that distort the moment so that you can more clearly focus on the immediate situation.

End-of-Chapter Exercise: Identifying Beliefs and Expectations

Several psychologists have developed questionnaires to identify common schemas that developed from the patterns between you and your childhood caretakers (Benjamin et al. 2006; Young, Klosko, and Weishaar 2003). Even when you are an adult and can choose the people you want to be intimate with, the core beliefs established in childhood may continue to influence your thinking and expectations.

In this exercise, underline how you think your parents would have most frequently responded. Then ask yourself if your philosophy of life or your typical way of responding to others is similar to the schema listed in the column on the far right.

If you...	Your caretakers would likely...	Possible Schema
Doubted your ability	Take over for you	You just can't do things well. You always need to know that someone is there, just in case.
	Criticize you	You are better off alone.
Needed reassurance	Make fun of your fears	You hate weakness in yourself or others. You don't trust anyone.
	Get impatient with you	You avoid asking for help.
Didn't do well enough	Blame the circumstances	You feel better than others. You blame others easily.
	Criticize you	You always push to prove yourself. You make excuses and avoid criticism. You seek approval from others.
Felt left out	Ignore you	You fear that no one will ever like you. You keep tabs on family and friends.

As children, we all had moments when we doubted our ability, needed help or reassurance from an adult, failed to live up to standards, or were excluded. It is impossible to pass through childhood without experiencing each of these situations. In vulnerable moments, our schemas become the lenses that make us interpret a situation a particular way. The feelings that were part of the earlier experience convince us that the same uncomfortable thing is happening again. When this happens, our expectations and response take over *before* we honestly understand exactly what is unfolding at the moment.

If you can identify the beliefs and expectations that were created in your childhood, then you are in a better position to notice when old lenses are coloring the way you are viewing the present. Your emotional response will be extremely familiar to you, especially if it is disturbing or uncomfortable.

Once you become aware that an old emotional schema has been activated, you are in a better position to prevent an overreaction. Just knowing that your interpretation may not be entirely accurate can help you in a number of ways. Rather than letting yourself go with the flow, you can step back and focus on returning to a balanced position. Techniques to help you do that will be explained in chapter 12, but the ability to identify the beliefs that make you vulnerable are a vital part of this skill. Once you have identified an old schema, you have developed the ability to challenge it on the grounds that it belongs to the past. As you will see in subsequent chapters, we can choose to challenge our thoughts in order to find better ways of responding.

CHAPTER 4

Family Values and Expectations

As much as we are shaped by the experiences that are captured in schemas, our identities are also influenced by aspects of our family life that have established our values. There is an old saying that "children become what they see," and to some extent, this seems to be true. *Tacit knowledge* refers to unspoken beliefs that we simply assume are held by everyone. We take these assumptions for granted, and when we encounter people who have different beliefs, we typically believe that they are wrong. Although there are different theories that explain how beliefs get passed down from generation to generation, the one that influences my own thinking about this has been developed by psychoanalysts.

Identification

Over the past fifty years, several psychoanalysts, such as W. W. Meissner (1980, 1986), have written on the subject of identity formation. Basically, they believe that we are strongly affected by our relationships and early interactions with our parents. When we are very young, we need to have a physical connection to feel secure. One of the challenges of going to school is being able to remind ourselves of our parents' availability when they are out of sight. If you have ever seen a child clinging to a favorite stuffed animal or blanket, you have observed what analysts call a transitional object: the stuffed animal or blanket helps remind the child that her loving parents have not disappeared forever and that she will be reunited with them in a few short hours. As she matures, she will find a way to keep that mental image and belief within her, so that by the time she turns six, she won't need her blanket very often; she will have found a different way to connect with the power of her parents' protection. Although she initially needed to see her parents or be held in order to feel safe, in time she is able to re-create the feeling of being safe by seeing or holding her blanket. Eventually, she shifts to a mental reference that brings the same sense of relief for her whenever she feels frightened or lonely.

We all have these internalized images of people who are important to us. What is even more fascinating, though, is that, over time, some of the qualities of these internalized images "leak" into our sense of self. Characteristics and values that we originally absorbed to preserve a sense of connection eventually become a permanent part of the way we experience ourselves. As time passes, we may not even realize that many aspects of our personality or outlook on life are unconsciously borrowed from the people who raised us.

Core Values

The process of identification helps explain how we acquire values and expectations for ourselves and the new families that we create. Often they become the core of our tacit knowledge, the things that we "just know." Although we typically reevaluate some of these values and expectations as we enter adolescence, many are never questioned or challenged.

During my years of experience working with families, it has always been interesting to see how a person who is the product of one family environment manages to adjust to another person whose tacit knowledge was created in a very different context. Even two people who share similar ethnic, religious, socioeconomic, and neighborhood backgrounds will have fundamental values and expectations that differ. Many of these beliefs are tested as the young couple struggles to establish the family rituals that will define them as they create their own home. Nesting brings many of these tacit beliefs to the foreground as the couple establishes their own customs and routines. Their expectations regarding religion, meals, purchases, and time spent with family, friends, or alone must be negotiated as things they took for granted are questioned or challenged by partners whose expectations and assumptions may be very different. Often, a couple must grapple with core assumptions and expectations that emerge when they become new parents and realize the importance of the core values that they want to instill in their children.

■ MARISSA AND CAMERON'S STORY

Marissa and Cameron felt blessed when, after five frustrating years of trying to have children, they brought home their healthy twin boys. When it came to preparing a nursery and choosing a pediatrician, the couple had arrived at decisions in a supportive and productive way. But Marissa really lost it when Cameron unpacked a box of presents her parents had shipped to them. Some of them were appropriate for infants, but others were intended to be used as the boys grew older. Marissa's parents had sent several expensive outfits and toys. As each gift was unwrapped, Cameron shook his head in disapproval and insisted that Marissa put all of the toys that required batteries back in the box. "I don't want my boys to be spoiled, and I don't want them to get used to these kinds of things. Children need to be able to construct things for themselves and use their imagination. Tell your parents to take these back and just get the boys blocks."

Marissa knew that Cameron's family had less money than her family and that Cameron had put himself through college. But her parents had good intentions and wanted to show their love for their grandchildren in ways that were similar to how they had raised her. Marissa thought that Cameron was being pushy, unreasonable, and unkind to her family. She snapped at him that the toys were going to stay whether he liked it or not.

Although Marissa and Cameron shared many values about raising children, Marissa was comfortable with luxury items and the latest gadgets. Her own memories of having these kinds of toys were familiar and pleasurable to her. Cameron, on the other hand, had worked at a country club throughout high school. He had seen families with money spoil their children with unnecessary indulgences. Cameron felt that those kinds of families looked down on hardworking families like his, and he had watched pampered infants turn into demanding brats who ended up being careless with property and unappreciative. Just as keeping the presents filled Marissa with a sense of continuity, the luxury items filled Cameron with horror. Both reactions were based on tacit assumptions formed in childhood.

Disidentification

Part of the process of becoming independent from our parents is recognizing the things about us that are unique and different. Even if we loved our parents dearly, there were probably certain things about them or the way they treated each other that we hated. I have worked with many people who recall being horrified by their parents' tempers or ashamed by the way their parents behaved in front of others. They recalled that, as children, they had silently vowed never to act that way when they grew up. The act of recoiling against a parent's values and deciding to do things differently forms the basis of *disidentification*. The passion to not become like your parents can be a powerful force in shaping values and expectations (J. P. Siegel 2004).

Although most of us would like to believe that choosing to do things differently is a big improvement, the pressure to be "opposite" is quite a burden. Even when we are deeply committed to living up to a certain standard, there are occasions when it is almost impossible to carry it out. While we all feel badly when we compromise our own standards and values, when we do something that violates a disidentification, we are often thrown out of emotional equilibrium.

For example, if you felt that your parents were disinterested in your schoolwork or after-school activities, you might vow to become the kind of parent who is always there for your children. But inevitably there will be times when you just can't be in two places at once. Even a mother with the best intentions will have conflicting responsibilities that prevent her from being at every event her children request. While most of us would feel bad to have to disappoint a child, those of us who have taken the vow of prioritizing our children's need for attention would have an extreme emotional reaction. Whether such a parent ends up getting frantic and rescheduling everything or simply shuts down, the intensity of the reaction has much more to do with the power of disidentification than the reality of the situation.

Successful adult coping requires flexibility and a wide range of options. When we are tied into behavior that is the opposite of a despised trait, we get locked into a very narrow frame, which usually makes us feel unbearably anxious or angry if we can't pull it off. We may also be highly reactive to the despised trait in others and may overreact when we find it in other people who can influence a shared outcome at home or at work. Often, we felt powerless in childhood to demand change from the adults who cared for us. But when we find the same objectionable traits in our adult relationships, we protest in a way that goes far beyond what the situation calls for.

■ SANDRA AND BRIAN'S STORY

Sandra and Brian started dating in high school and, for the most part, had a successful marriage. While Sandra tended to be volatile and impulsive, Brian was calm and predictable, and both were pleased with the balance they brought to their shared life. The only thing that displeased Sandra was Brian's tendency to do things in ways that often fell below her expectations. While she didn't expect that he would always do everything perfectly, she found herself getting furious when she saw him putting something off that she had asked him to do. From Brian's point of view, Sandra seemed to go crazy every time he wanted to relax. She made him feel that watching a game on TV or taking a nap on a Sunday afternoon was a sin.

In therapy, I asked Sandra about her parents' marriage and about which parent had been the more demanding. Sandra immediately answered that her parents were actually very similar and that they both could let things go without getting too distressed. Sandra grew up thinking that everyone made mashed potatoes from a packaged mix and that furniture scratches or stains couldn't be repaired. In contrast, both of her maternal grandparents seemed to be more focused on achievement. She could tell that her grandparents were deeply disappointed in the way their daughter managed her life and that they were closer to their other children. As Sandra grew older and spent time at her friends' houses, her embarrassment about her own parents grew. In time, Sandra judged her parents to be lazy and felt that their style of accepting the easy way out had held the whole family back. She set higher standards for herself and vowed to create a family life that was based on higher standards than she had grown up with.

Her grandparents had helped pay for Sandra's college tuition and seemed proud of her good grades. Sandra got engaged to her high school boyfriend in her final year of college. In part, her attraction to Brian was based on his intelligence and ambition and the shared values they would carry forward.

Although Sandra could acknowledge that everyone was entitled to relax sometimes, she found it almost impossible not to react when Brian settled into his spot in front of the TV. Sandra's overreaction contain a mix of identification and disidentification. Sandra would find herself overcome by irritability and disapproval that was related to a belief that Brian was somehow complacent or lazy. Without realizing it, she feared that Brian was just like her parents and that his laziness would take over their shared life. To Sandra, a man who could be content with the substandard would never be someone she could respect or genuinely partner with. The urgency of the situation was based on a fear that if she let one thing slide, their entire family would tumble into a sea of mediocrity.

Self-Knowledge

The values and beliefs that we grow up with often hold tremendous power over us. Many of the triggers that set off an overreaction have a connection to our childhood experiences. By understanding the identifications and disidentifications that define us, we are able to better understand why certain themes tend to upset us. In the middle of an emotional reaction, we don't have the ability to analyze the tacit beliefs that have been activated. However, knowing which issues are our own personal hot buttons helps us recognize them when the thoughts and feelings are awakened. Later in this book, I will help you consider ways to loosen the power of old beliefs, but the first step is to understand the themes that make you vulnerable to overreacting.

End-of-Chapter Exercise: How Well Do You Know Yourself?

In the following exercise, I will refer to those who raised you as your mother and father, regardless of whether they are biological, step-, or adoptive parents, or important figures in your upbringing. I use the term "marriage" whether your parents are or were partners or married. If you experienced more than one parental marriage during your childhood, you can jot down your answers for all that you remember. If you were raised in a single-parent home, just answer the questions that apply to your childhood. You don't need to restrict your response or feel bad if you leave questions blank. I will be asking you to refer to your answers here to do other parts of these exercises, so I encourage you to write down the answers to these questions in a notebook or journal, as there is just too much information to remember.

Part 1

Think about your family when you were growing up. Jot down the first thing that comes to your mind to complete each of these phrases:

- In thinking about my parents, the thing I most respected about my mother was the way she...

- The thing I most respected about my father was the way he...

- In thinking about my parents' marriage, the thing they did the best or handled extremely well was...

- When I think about my mother, the one trait that most embarrassed or turned me off was...

- When I think about my father, the one trait that most embarrassed or turned me off was...

- In thinking about my parents' marriage, the thing that made me most uncomfortable was...

- If I could have changed one thing about my mother, I would have made her...

- If I could have changed one thing about my father, I would have made him...

Part 2

Now highlight or underline the key words and themes that appear in each of your responses and answer the following questions:

- Do you see any of these characteristics in yourself or in your most important relationships?

- Write down one of your likenesses to either parent that fills you with comfort or pride.

- Write down one of your likenesses to either parent that makes you uncomfortable or ashamed.

- What recent situation made you aware of this unwanted trait?

- Would this kind of situation typically lead to an emotional overreaction?

Although there are certain situations that can provoke overreactions for most people, the personal values that you have acquired play a very important role in defining the issues you are most sensitive to. By taking the time to think about the qualities that you observed and reacted to in your childhood family, you will be more quickly alerted when these core values are challenged. You may still end up doing what feels "right," but you will be able to recognize the identifications and disidentifications that are stimulating your response.

CHAPTER 5

Splitting, Denial, and Flooding

When we are overcome by emotions, our ability to see things objectively is thrown out the window. Even when we switch to the logical left brain, our emotional system is on overload and will automatically attempt to reduce our levels of anxiety and tension. To do this, psychological defense mechanisms spring into action. A *defense mechanism* is an unconscious response to anxiety that allows us to deal with the situation from a safer position. Just as a suit of armor will deflect an arrow, a defense mechanism temporarily alters the way we view the situation that has made us feel overwhelmed. When our central nervous system just can't handle another difficult moment, our defense mechanisms come to the rescue.

Psychological Defense Mechanisms

You have probably heard about some of the more common defense mechanisms and, if you have studied psychology, may even know which ones you tend to use. Many of us use *rationalization* when we want to justify why we can bend the rules when it suits us. Most of us use *sublimation*, which allows us to harness energy that cannot be safely released and turn it into something more productive. For example, if a friend has made you so furious that you would like to punch him in the face, you might decide to grab the garden shears and trim down some overgrown bushes instead.

When it comes to overreacting, various defense mechanisms join forces. Perhaps the most important defense is one referred to in the psychological field as *splitting*. Under the influence of splitting, we see things in an exaggerated fashion. Things are either all good or all bad. However, in order to see things in such an extreme way, the defense mechanism of *denial* automatically kicks in. When we are emotionally centered, things are rarely entirely good or completely bad. However, in order to preserve a perspective based on splitting, denial acts like a pair of blinders that prevents us from noticing or giving much credence to anything that would contradict a one-sided opinion. To put this another way, if splitting requires that we see something as completely black, denial makes sure that anything white or gray is kept out of sight and out of mind. As a result, we are only able to recognize certain aspects of a situation and end up seeing things in a skewed manner. Not having all the information available makes it more likely that our reactions and decisions will not be the best ones possible.

Splitting not only obscures our judgment, it also adds to the intensity of our experience. As if that isn't bad enough, the combination of splitting and denial often stimulates memories of other situations that were experienced in the extreme. When this happens, we are *flooded* by old memories and all of the feelings that were experienced in the past. These emotional memories and leftover emotions from the past comingle with the present situation in a way that magnifies our response. Splitting, denial, and flooding can be activated in less than thirty seconds, creating an appraisal and an intense response that have little to do with the situation at hand (J. P. Siegel 1992, 2006).

■ JENNY'S STORY

Jenny's resentment toward her husband Phil had been growing for two years, but one night she exploded and was ready to call the marriage quits. Jenny had worked late and was exhausted by the time she got home. She had been relieved to see Phil's car in the driveway. She hated to think that the girls were home alone. True, they were responsible girls who were more than capable of heating up the dinner she had left for them, but lately Kristen had been slacking off on her homework.

But instead of finding the girls doing their work and the house running smoothly, the sight that greeted Jenny made her wish she had stayed even longer at work. The kitchen was a mess, with orange peels and peanut shells all over the counter tops. Phil was zoned out in front of the TV, completely oblivious to the mess, the girls, or the fact that the dog was lapping water from the toilet. But she really lost it when she called upstairs to ask Kristen if she was doing her homework and Phil interjected. When Phil told her to leave Kristen alone, she felt like he was working against her. Instead of having a partner who shared her concern for their children, she had a third teenager who just wanted to play his way through life. Not only was he setting a bad example for their daughters, he was intervening to protect them from her. The look on his face made her feel that he was judging her as being too serious, demanding, and difficult. Of course the girls would rather chat on the Internet than do their homework, and of course they would prefer the parent who let them get away with things. It became perfectly clear that not only would she never get the support she needed, she would have to work twice as hard to put out the fires that Phil was setting.

If we take a closer look at this situation, it is easy to see splitting in action. When Jenny saw Phil relaxing despite the disarray in the kitchen, her mind came to several rapid conclusions. From her perspective, Phil was once again being completely irresponsible. Without being aware of it, Jenny flashed back to other situations that, in her opinion, Phil had mismanaged. While Jenny prided herself on living up to her commitments, Phil could often let things slide. Jenny immediately assumed that this was just another example of Phil allowing himself to tune out the girls in order to relax. Splitting brought Jenny to a rapid assessment that colored her judgment and reaction. Now that she was focused on Phil's inadequacies, she immediately assumed that Phil had not adequately supervised Kristen and that, in all likelihood, Kristen was goofing off. Because she didn't feel that Phil was supporting her, Jenny believed that Phil was undermining her and encouraging the girls to choose pleasure over responsibility.

But Jenny hadn't even taken the time to find out whether Kristen's homework was done and what had been going on prior to her arrival that made Phil tell her to back off. Splitting had led to a very specific vantage point, and she had filled in the blanks with her own version of the truth.

All Good or All Bad

While it is perfectly normal to use personal history to inform our understanding of current realities, splitting directs us to stored memories that do not relate fully to the present situation. One way to understand how splitting works is to imagine a two-drawer filing cabinet. Memories are not just randomly accumulated but are attached to schemas that are organized before they are filed away. Splitting separates our positive schemas from ones that are filled with pain or disappointment. In the memory cabinet that we each have, we store the positive memories and schemas in one drawer and the memories of things that we wish had never happened in the other. But it is impossible to have both drawers open at the same time. If a schema from the good drawer is activated, the entire drawer may slide open. When that happens, we are focused only on the good and have no awareness or access to things that are tucked away in the bad drawer. In a similar way, when a schema from the bad drawer is opened, we become aware of other emotional memories filed in that drawer. At the same time, the schemas about good things that could have offset or balanced the bad are, for the moment, tightly sealed away in the good drawer. When we only have access to memories that are either all good or all bad, we are primed to overreact.

Drs. Lorna Benjamin and F. J. Friedrich (1991) suggest that the feelings that are awakened when memory schemas are activated can be very intense. The schemas also carry our conclusions about past experiences. Without realizing it, this colors our expectations, as it is normal to assume that what happened before might happen again.

In the story above, Jenny has a file that is dedicated to the subject of competence. In fact, there are two files dedicated to competence: one is located in the good drawer, and the other is filed in the bad drawer. If Jenny had opened the file labeled "Feeling proud of Phil," she would be flooded with pride and security. She would likely remember how Phil was recognized as salesman of the year and was celebrated at last year's company banquet. She might remember how clever he had been when he installed a speaker system that required an amazing amount of patience. But seeing Phil relaxed despite the orange peels and peanut shells had stimulated a schema of incompetence and pushed Jenny into the drawer of bad experiences. All she could think about were Phil's shortcomings and failures, from a file labeled "Phil screws up again."

Once the bad drawer is open, the situation is ripe for overreaction. Because Jenny was flooded with memories of past incidents where Phil's low standards had caused her to be shamed or compromised, she assumed that this time would be no different. She expected that Phil would come up with some lame excuse as he had done in the past or turn it around and blame her for not making her expectations clear. She started to feel utterly pessimistic that life with Phil could ever make her happy. In ten seconds, Jenny's thoughts had gone from the orange peels to memories of twenty years of accumulated failings. Denial prevented Jenny from asking whether the girls had finished their homework and from noticing that aside from the signs of a late-night snack, all the dinner dishes had been cleaned and put away.

As we get to know the file cabinets that can rule our emotional lives, we will notice that the files in each of the drawers are not ordered alphabetically. Some files are located so close to other files that when one is accessed, others get pulled out as well. In Jenny's case, her experience of needing to defend her standards against Phil led to the possibility of conflict with a close family member. The recognition of differences between them had opened the file in the bad drawer labeled "Criticism leads to losing love." When Phil told her to back off, Jenny felt threatened that she would be excluded from the bond shared by her husband and children. If a therapist had been there to probe the past, Jenny might have remembered times when her parents criticized and then rejected her. There might also have been times when friends disapproved of how she had handled something and excluded her from their circle. But at that moment, it was Phil joining with her daughters in a shared defiance against her. While the details of this scenario were different, once the files from the past had sprung open, the combination of flooding, splitting, and denial created the straw that broke the camel's back.

When we are in an episode where we are splitting and flooding, the present situation becomes even more unbearable. As the past merges with the present, it is impossible for us to untangle the different sources of feelings. The intensity and certainty that we feel in the moment may be our only clues that our response might be far greater than the immediate situation calls for.

It is always easier to recognize splitting after the fact. When the incident has passed, we have room to consider alternative explanations and concede to misunderstandings. But when we are in the midst of splitting, our confused emotions create a sense of truth and certainty that justifies emotions that are in many ways blinding. If you find yourself in an intense situation that seems totally one-sided, you are probably splitting and flooding. Our relationships are rarely completely good or totally bad. Sometimes being aware that you have taken an all-or-nothing stance is the first clue that splitting and flooding have taken over. When we see things as all good or all bad, we have opened the file cabinet and found a schema that causes us to view things through a lens that narrows our view. Even the people and things that we hate the most have some good points, and in most situations there are some positives to offset the negatives. When things seem to point in only one direction, splitting is most likely the culprit. Denial makes sure that we only focus on aspects that will reinforce our perspective, leading us to interpret events through a lens that skews our perspective. Our response seems perfectly justified and appropriate to us but way out of line to everyone else.

End-of-Chapter Exercises

The folders that you have in the drawers of your file cabinet are unique to you, but knowing about the common themes and triggers (described in section 2) might shed light on those issues or triggers that are powerful enough to open your "bad" drawer and cause you to overreact.

Exercise 1: In My Family

Families that operate with a high level of splitting can generate this kind of response pattern in their children. Look at each of the descriptions and patterns listed in this exercise and note whether each was true or false in your family.

True or false: In the family in which I grew up...

- we never knew when a small problem would turn into a crisis.

- some days my parents thought I was great; other days, they thought I was terrible.

- people saw things the way they wanted to, not how they were.

- people frequently exaggerated.

- our parents would punish one of us for something that another sibling could get away with.

- my mother or father could stay in a bad mood for days on end.

- someone would mention problems from the past during arguments.

- people believed what they wanted to believe regardless of evidence to the contrary.

If you answered "true" to most of these questions, then chances are you grew up with defensive splitting. If that is the case, it means that you had less exposure to ways of handling problems in calm, thoughtful ways. Families who operate out of the "all good" or "all bad" drawer frequently generate this style of reacting in their children. Learning to identify those of your triggers that most often stimulate splitting and recognizing what your intense posture feels like will help you de-escalate a cycle that has the potential to harm you and the people you are close to.

Exercise 2: Identifying Splitting

Although there are some triggers and schemas that are more common than others, you need to know exactly what yours look and feel like. When you are splitting, there are specific thoughts, beliefs, expectations, feelings, and responses that tend to be repeated. I will start you out in this exercise by listing responses that are common. You can think about whether each is true or false for you. I hope it will get you to start thinking about the specific thoughts and responses that you experience when you are in *your* "good" and "bad" drawers so that you can jot them down in your notebook. Now that you know what splitting is, you will notice it in almost every story of people I have worked with over the years. If any of these examples make you aware of your own tendencies to do the same thing, add those insights to your notebook.

True or false: When I am in my good drawer...

- I get excited by what I think is going to happen next.

- I feel a huge relief from the worries I usually have.

- I don't want anything to bring me down.

- I want to keep things just like this for as long as I can.

- I don't want to hear about any problems.

True or false: When I am in my bad drawer...

- I feel outraged that I have been treated this badly.

- I feel pessimistic or even hopeless that things will ever change.

- I doubt that anyone is going to fix this or help me.

- It's difficult to think about anything good.

- I feel terrible about myself and everyone who is part of this mess.

- I think this situation is incredibly unfair and blame someone for making it happen.

It is important for you to remember that splitting is a state. Psychologists emphasize the difference between a *state*, which is a temporary way of being, and a *trait*, which is something inherent in us. Just as our thoughts and feelings shift when we enter a certain state, they shift again when we leave it. Chapter 12 will give you more ideas to help you confront and diminish an episode of splitting, but the earlier you can recognize your thoughts, feelings, and physical responses, the easier it will be to regain your perspective.

SECTION 2

The Triggers

Overreactions never occur in a vacuum. We all have childhood experiences that can complicate the way we interpret and respond to an event, even if we are not consciously aware of them. Some similarity between the previous event and the current one can cause old emotional memories and beliefs to spring into action, setting off a chain of physical and emotional reactions. How well do you know the situations that make you most likely to overreact?

While we all have our own areas of sensitivity, there are some situations that seem to evoke a strong emotional response for most people. In this section, I invite you to learn more about four themes that are almost universal in their potential to evoke strong emotional reactions—envy, rejection, criticism, and control. While this is not an all-inclusive list, these themes have been a focus in clinical publications as well as research and have been hot buttons for many of the clients I have worked with over the past thirty years. I hope that you will look at these themes not as faults or weaknesses but as issues that affect many people. Understanding the power of these triggers will put you in a better position to recognize what is happening before your emotions get the best of you. As you read about the ways that other people have responded, ask yourself if you have ever reacted in similar ways. The more you know about the situations that make you the most vulnerable, the better prepared you will be to notice and attend to the earliest signals of an unprocessed emotional response.

CHAPTER 6

Envy

Envy is a very powerful human emotion that can be experienced by all people regardless of age, religion, or cultural background. Despite its importance, only a handful of psychologists have chosen to study it, and they can't seem to agree completely on what it is or what exactly causes it.

Defining Envy

Although most of us know what envy feels like, it is easy to confuse an episode of envy and an experience of jealousy. Most experts in the field think that there are important differences (Smith and Kim 2007). We feel *jealous* when someone threatens to take something or someone we already have. We feel *envious* when someone gets something that we want and think we deserve. In a typical episode of envy, we feel angry. When we start thinking about the situation, we have a sense of injustice, based on our view that it isn't fair. Sometimes there is an uncomfortable sense of being deprived, and sometimes we might even hope that the person we envy gets hurt or fails. Thinking about the situation usually makes us feel worse, as, at the end of the day, we feel powerless to change it. So in an episode of envy, we usually experience some degree of anger, injustice, deprivation, powerlessness, and a desire for the other to fail.

Part of the reason that envy is so difficult to understand is that it is a socially undesirable quality. Most of us feel uncomfortable admitting to feeling envious when something good happens to someone we know at work or in our family. Why is it so difficult to acknowledge this important emotion? Most religions preach against envy, and some religious teaching has left us feeling that it is a sin to covet what another person has. In many cultures, there are superstitions to ward off the power of envy and the evil that those who have less might wish upon others. The idea that wishing harm on someone might have the power to make that harm happen causes people to stay away from the whole experience. Those of us who grew up with siblings also know that parents tend to be impatient and disapproving if we protest that a sister or brother is being favored. When parents, teachers, religious leaders, and cultural influences work in concert to tell us that it is bad to feel envious, most of us learn to keep quiet or even feel guilty for feeling that way.

Situations That Create Envy

Although most of us admire the lifestyles of the rich and famous, we usually don't go around flooded with envy every time we see them on TV or read about them in a magazine. We are much more likely to envy people who are or are almost our equals. We become envious when we believe that they have received or obtained something that will make them better off than we are or will improve their lives in important ways.

Sometimes we feel envious about material goods, but there are many other categories that stimulate envy. In fact, if you asked twenty people what things they have envied, you might get twenty different answers. Someone who feels bad about her figure and struggles to keep her weight down might envy her best friend, who stays thin no matter what she eats. Someone else might envy a coworker who shows off a new watch or car that seems impossible to afford. It is not uncommon for stay-at-home moms to envy women who seem to have interesting jobs, while working moms envy those who get to spend the whole day with their children. A person who is showing signs of aging may envy an old friend who looks years younger, while a person who hates his job might envy a colleague who announces his plan to retire at the end of the year.

When we feel that someone else is much better off because that person received something that could have been given to us, it is hard not to feel envious. Research shows that when a person feels that she has been treated unfairly, her amygdala is activated (Crockett 2009). Competition and the desire not to be left behind stimulate emotions that are intense and uncomfortable. When this is coupled with a sense of unfairness, it is almost impossible not to respond. No one likes to feel "less than," and no one likes to feel powerless to change it.

■ PATRICE'S STORY

Patrice had discovered Pilates in her midtwenties and had a natural talent and a strong interest in it. After advancing to a high level, she took classes that would prepare her to become a Pilates instructor. One of her friends, Alice, took advanced classes with her and was interested in her experiences in the instructor's training program. Often, they would go out for lunch after class, and Patrice encouraged her friend to consider the training. By the time Alice decided to enroll, Patrice was teaching three classes at their studio and enjoying every minute of it.

But things changed very quickly after Alice graduated from the training program. At first, Alice was very appreciative when Patrice let her be the substitute instructor when she had to miss a class. But Patrice would often find Alice hanging around the studio owner's office, volunteering to do things and complimenting her on every occasion. Soon Alice was invited to substitute teach other classes, including an advanced class that Patrice doubted Alice could handle. One day, when they went to lunch, Alice started to eagerly list all of the classes she had been asked to sub and mentioned that the owner was thinking about offering her an intermediate level class at a prime time. Patrice felt such an intense stab of envy that she couldn't eat another mouthful. That class was one that she had been promised, and it was only offered to seasoned instructors. To think that Alice could be offered a plum class without having to prove herself was unbelievable. Patrice knew that it was more about Alice's hanging around and throwing out compliments than about her talent or skill and was enraged that her boss had been stupid enough to fall for it. She felt betrayed for having been helpful to Alice and furious that she was supposed to just sit there and congratulate someone who was getting something she didn't deserve at all.

Identifying Envy

You know you are envious when you think...

- it doesn't seem fair that other people have an easier time getting the things you want.

- it is annoying to see people who don't deserve it advance.

- you're the one doing the hard work while someone else is getting rewarded.

- other people have all the luck.

- you can't count blessings because other people have so much more.

- it's not fair for other people to get sympathy for things that you have gone through with little support.

- it's not fair when people get the things that you want and they don't even appreciate it.

- it's not right for everyone to make a fuss over someone else, while you're taken for granted.

Envy is a normal response that is difficult to acknowledge. When we can accept that it is a powerful trigger for most people, we can allow ourselves to spend more time understanding the feelings, beliefs, and impulses that have been generated.

Envy in the Family

Envy would not exist if there was perfect equality and an abundance of everything that anyone could ever want. Unfortunately, such a utopia doesn't exist, and we learn this at a very young age. If you have children or are in a position to observe family interactions, you will see how intensely children want to possess the most precious resource in their life—their mother. Freud, considering envy in boys, thought that little boys developed penis envy when they realized that they had to share their mother's love with the "other man" in her life. Freud also thought that little boys had wild imaginations and wished they could kill their fathers and, at the same time, were afraid that their fathers (who were stronger and more powerful than they were) would find out about their wishes and retaliate by chopping off their penises. Although Freud was considering envy only in boys, the cycle that he identified, in which envy leads to aggressive impulses that then lead to a fear of retaliation followed by guilt, is a common psychological experience.

When I teach my social work students about this pattern, someone usually points out that Freud's explanation is more about jealousy than envy. After all, the child is trying to possess his mother and doesn't want her taken by someone else. But Freud says that we are shocked to learn that our mothers don't really belong to us and that they are more interested in the grown-up companions they had before we ever came along. The combination of feeling both deprived and powerless to change the status quo is a powerful introduction to envy.

Sibling Rivalry

Family therapists have also observed how early childhood relationships plant the seeds of envy, but they are more interested in the way things develop between siblings. The idea of sibling rivalry is probably something you are already familiar with. Although kids may seem to be fighting over who gets to ride in the front seat of the car or who gets the slice of cake with the most icing, most therapists agree that what kids are really competing for is their parents' love. All children want to be the center of attention and hope that they are their parents' favorite. When a parent pays more attention to a sister or brother, the illusion of being special is shattered.

Competing against a sibling is usually a no-win situation, because when children turn to their parents to protest, they rarely get what they want. Most parents are annoyed when their children bicker, and disapprove of how strongly kids fight over such small prizes. The child who is flooded with envy usually winds up feeling left out, diminished, treated unfairly, and powerless to change it.

Ultimately, children learn to take things into their own hands. Some children believe that even if they are powerless to change one scenario, the game isn't over. This kind of child will try to take revenge on the sibling who got the preferential treatment by using physical or emotional tactics such as breaking a favorite toy or refusing to let the sibling join in play. Another child might figure out that she can do other things to get the attention she craves, even if it means getting sick or failing.

Although it happens less frequently, occasionally one parent has a need to get the most attention in the family. This is usually a reaction to that parent's experience of not getting enough attention in childhood and not wanting to share it now. Without realizing it, a parent may become very envious of the attention lavished on a child and feel irritable or miserable for vague reasons. This kind of envy is very difficult to acknowledge but leads to different forms of competition with children for affirmation and attention. I have worked with fathers who feel displaced when a first child is born but don't want to acknowledge feelings of anger or loss. It is even worse when everyone is congratulating them and they end up feeling guilty for being angry at all the changes in their lives. Just as often, a mother can be made uncomfortable by the attention that is lavished on others in the family.

■ GINA'S STORY

By the age of thirty, Gina was happily married to Carl and enjoying a challenging but rewarding career in software development. The problem was Gina's difficulty keeping friends, including couples who wanted to include Gina and Carl in a social network that was important to Carl. Gina's tendency to cancel plans at the last minute or forget to respond to invitations led to fights and tension at home. Gina admitted that she liked almost every person who wanted to befriend them and enjoyed having lunch or going for walks on a one-to-one basis. But when four or more friends came together, she just couldn't handle it.

When I asked Gina to tell me about her family, she expressed considerable anger and resentment toward her mother. She described her mother as a demanding, selfish woman who used everyone to her own benefit. As Gina started to tell me stories to illustrate her perceptions, she shared that the worst thing was when she tried to bring her friends home. Instead of letting the girls hang out or play by themselves, Gina's mother had to be the center of attention. She would zero in on Gina's friends, telling stories and starting conversations that would completely leave Gina out. Soon, her friends would be laughing at her mother's jokes and completely ignoring Gina. In therapy, Gina was able to understand how she had envied and resented her mother's charm and wit. It made her aware of her own more serious nature and how awkward she felt when she had to initiate conversation. But the strongest feeling was anger and resentment that her mother had been intruding on Gina's friendships to get her own needs met.

As she thought about it, she realized that Carl also had an ease and comfort socializing with friends. The tendency for the most energized conversation and laughter to focus around Carl created a sense of envy that was intolerable to Gina. Once Gina recognized how her unresolved resentment toward her mother could easily be stimulated and then misplaced onto Carl, Gina was able to keep those feelings in the past and join in the fun with a sense of pride in her husband.

Childhood Coping Styles

How you reacted to envy when you were a child predicts how you will react as an adult. Some children learn to use personal power and become assertive. To make sure they will get their fair share the next time, they become increasingly competitive and watchful. However, their impulses may also be vengeful and extremely aggressive, which can occur in children before their moral guidelines are fully matured. Other children might object a few times to unfair situations but ultimately feel worse for trying to get what they want. Focusing on wanting something and being powerless to get it can be a source of deep pain. For example, a little girl might realize that her father will never enjoy throwing the ball with her, even though he seems to love doing that with her brother. Even though it's not fair, she realizes that she can't do anything to change his mind or to prove that she is good enough to join in. Rather than become more competitive or assertive, she may enter into a cycle of self-doubt and withdrawal. Children who feel neglected often experience this more profoundly than adults do, partially because they fear that any anger they express against the parent who has caused the initial disappointment will create even more problems. As a result, the child experiences personal failure and helplessness that add to the level of despair.

■ CATHY AND SID'S STORY

Cathy and Sid came to me for marital therapy, complaining that they were fighting all the time. Part of the problem was Cathy's resentment that Sid wasn't financially successful. He was easily distracted at home and at work and tended to gloss over things that were important to his business dealings. Cathy had quit her job after their first child was born and was glad that she had been able to put energy into raising three boys who had an assortment of problems, including food allergies and attention deficit disorder. But after Sid lost yet another job, she decided it was more important to return to work on a full-time basis.

One day, Cathy called me in desperation. Things at her job were hectic, and she had to work overtime. She hadn't arranged for the sitter to stay late because she was counting on leaving promptly. Tonight was the boy's school music recital, and they had been practicing their pieces all week. At first she was relieved when Sid told her he had it under control, but suddenly she felt furious at him. He was the one whose business was slow enough for him to leave early, while she was the one overloaded with deadlines. He got to enjoy the concert and take the boys out for their traditional ice cream celebration while she was scurrying to catch a commuter train that might get her home in time to at least tuck them in before they fell asleep. It just felt completely unfair that while she was working extra hard to make sure that there was money for instruments and ice cream, Sid was the one who had the pleasure of enjoying the concert and the ice cream to boot. She felt resentful that he got to enjoy something she wanted so badly and that the kids would have yet another memory of sharing a celebration with their happy, relaxed father, while their serious mother was out of sight and out of mind.

This was a horrible feeling for Cathy to bear, as it reminded her too much of how her own mother had acted after her parents divorced. Cathy had hated when her mother accused her of taking her father's side and loving her father more. The more her mother complained and created tension, the more Cathy felt that she did prefer her father. At least he kept his feelings to himself and never put her in the middle. At the thought that she was turning into her mother, Cathy slipped into feelings of helplessness and depression. She had vowed that she would never become bitter and complaining, like her mother had been, and now she was being put into the same position.

It was easy for me to empathize with Cathy's feelings of being left out, powerless, and deprived for reasons that were completely unfair. But at first, Cathy disagreed when I commented, "Envy is such a difficult feeling." To Cathy, envy was unforgivable, and it made her feel ashamed that she had slipped that low. Not being able to admit to the emotion only made the problem more difficult to solve.

Envy at Work

It would be fair to say that competition breeds envy. Who wouldn't want to be acknowledged for doing an excellent job or given a promotion? Even when money isn't at stake, coworkers bristle when only one person is acknowledged or one person takes the credit for other people's work. Sometimes being appreciated and recognized is as important as a financial reward.

Just as your family had its own way of allowing or curtailing sibling rivalry, the company you work for has its own culture. Some organizations thrive on competition and believe that it brings out the best in people. While it is true that the desire to win creates inspiration and encourages attention to detail, there is an emotional cost that is rarely recognized. Just as some children become aggressive and retaliate against siblings, employees can turn against a coworker who is unfairly rewarded. Malicious envy at work can take many forms, including backstabbing, harmful gossip, and undercutting the "opponent" at every opportunity. Even when a coworker appears to be handling things maturely, he may be trying to sabotage his competition at every opportunity. If your work environment allows that kind of behavior, it is very difficult to maintain a sense of group cooperation. The confidence that comes from being part of a team goes out the window and is replaced by a sense of mistrust. Instead of being able to concentrate on the job, you may find that too much of your energy is wasted on interpersonal dynamics.

In the face of unguided competition, some people back away from the heat and withdraw. However, this response can be equally damaging to the work environment. Have you ever worked with someone who seems sour about your group or the entire company? Envying others can lead to feelings of being treated unfairly and being powerless to change a situation (Vecchio 2000). A person who believes she will never get the recognition or advancement that others get may feel resentful and demoralized. This kind of response can be contagious, as it cramps everyone's enthusiasm and expectation that a job well done will be rewarded. Working with someone who is pessimistic and cynical makes it difficult to maintain your own positive energy, as your efforts are made to seem a complete waste of time. An entire team can be brought down this way.

Tolerating Envy

A thoughtful response to envy involves recognizing the emotional experience as it unfolds. In response to the trigger, you might feel a sudden tension in your chest or stomach and become aware of muscles tightening in your neck, back, or hands. You might be aware of feeling angry, deprived, resentful, neglected, or diminished and find it difficult to focus on anything else. Rather than allowing your thoughts and feelings to take over, put your energy into getting centered. As you register the thoughts and feelings that have been created, acknowledge that you have been stimulated to feel envy.

To put the situation into perspective, scan for incidents from the past that may have resurfaced. When feelings are stronger than the immediate situation calls for, chances are you are flooded with old emotional memories. Some of your old beliefs and schemas are probably complicating or even distorting your appraisal and expectations.

Separating Past from Present

While the emotional memories that are in your file cabinet are unique to you, we all had childhood experiences that created envy. The better you understand your own sensitivities, the more quickly you can recognize a feeling from the past that has been reactivated. Once childhood memories spring into action, we start thinking and acting like we did when we were younger. When that happens, we strip ourselves of the power and ability we possess, as adults, to analyze a situation. The less clearly we understand the power of these past emotional memories, the more quickly they can invade the moment and add to the pain of the current experience.

Processing the Emotion of Envy

When you are in the middle of an episode that creates envy, the situation may seem intolerable. One way to manage this is to activate the thinking part of your brain along with the emotional part. Remember, your amygdala will lose power if you can become thoughtful and aware. To help accomplish this, consider these questions:

- Are you reacting mainly to the injustice? ("It isn't fair!")

- Are you reacting mainly to thinking you have no power? ("There's nothing I can do about it.")

- Are you reacting mainly to feeling left behind or left out? ("I never get the good stuff.")

Once you know which aspects of the situation disturb you the most, ask yourself if your point of view might be somewhat skewed. When we are in the middle of a situation, we usually lose sight of the bigger picture and give too much weight to the situation at hand. It often helps if we can reestablish our perspective.

Reestablishing Perspective

Part of solving your dilemma is trying to regain perspective. To do this, consider these questions:

- What are the things in life that you value the most? How does this incident relate to those key things?

- Are you blowing up the importance of something that, when all is considered, isn't that huge?

- Are you assuming that losing out one time will have permanent or irreversible consequences?

- Why do you believe that there will never be another opportunity to make things better for yourself?

- Are you splitting (seeing things as either all good or all bad)? Do you think that you *never* get the things you deserve or want? Are you only remembering the other times that you lost out and forgetting times that worked in your favor? Are you viewing the person you envy as *only* or *always* getting the good stuff?

Remember, envy is a normal emotion. It's not wrong to experience envy, but focusing on your situation in this way won't help you solve it. Once you identify that you are experiencing envy, you have taken the first step toward taking control of a response that can be damaging to you and others. Aggressive or malicious competition and cynical or helpless pessimism are painful and need to be challenged. If you let your childhood response style take over, you will lose the opportunity to use your feelings to solve the problem in a thoughtful way.

Being able to put things in perspective will help you calm down. Remember, the amygdala is activated when you perceive a threat. If you are flooded with old emotional memories, it is almost impossible to evaluate the present situation on its own.

When you are able to separate old schemas and memories from the present situation, your emotional intensity will diminish. However, the point of resolving an overreaction is not just to restore calm. Sometimes, envy awakens us to a problem that truly needs to change. When we are able to thoughtfully acknowledge how important something is, we can get out of a stuck position and consider different ways to create changes. Usually, we have more options than we are aware of in the middle of an intense emotional episode. Once you are able to calmly consider your situation, there may be lots of productive things that you can and should do.

Thoughtful Responses

Things that may help resolve a situation that produces envy include the following:

- Talk to other people who care and can offer support and encouragement. You are not just looking for sympathy but want to remember that there are people who truly care about you and your happiness.

- Identify a new goal or opportunity to get what you want. Once you identify that new target, give yourself a pep talk to generate confidence that it is doable.

- Evaluate whether you have been caught up in goals that were created by others versus values that you have defined for yourself. It is so easy to be influenced to want things that you really don't need and to forget that you have found a formula for contentment that works just fine for you.

- Finally, even though it may not seem related, spend time helping others who have less. Envy is quickly put into perspective when we see how truly lucky we are.

End-of-Chapter Exercises

It is almost impossible to grow up without experiencing childhood envy. Many of these deep emotional memories have been buried because they were too intense and uncomfortable for you to stay in touch with. As you think about your childhood, you may once again feel some of that original discomfort. Although this may be difficult, it is a worthwhile challenge if you take it in *small* steps. Remember, your body will signal you when you feel danger. If that happens to you during this exercise, or while you are reading any part of this book, stop reading and just jot down one sentence in your journal that captures what you were thinking; there will be time to return to any of the themes that are particularly difficult for you. Your goal is to learn ways of processing difficult emotions so that they lose the power they once held. You can choose how much to take on at any one time, knowing that it makes sense to become comfortable with a small emotional memory rather than allowing yourself to get flooded with too much information.

Exercise 1: Your Childhood Envy

To better understand your vulnerabilities, ask yourself the following questions. See if you can remember a specific incident that "proves" your point. Write down as much as you remember.

- What talents or attributes were most prized in your family? Where were you ranked?

- Did you get your fair share of recognition for other talents or attributes?

- What things could your siblings do better than you could? How were they rewarded?

- Who was your mother's favorite child? Why do you think that?

- Who was your father's favorite child? Why do you think that?

When you think about the details of past incidents, you unleash the emotional memories that accompany them. Don't be surprised or uncomfortable if envy was one of the feelings you experienced. I would like to give you permission to acknowledge the feeling of envy so that you can spend some time understanding it better. Ultimately, I would like to help you identify and challenge the ingredients of envy that are most painful for you. Perhaps you are uncomfortable with feeling powerless or deprived. Perhaps the response of wishing harm on someone you love makes you feel frightened or guilty. By exploring your unique response to childhood and family memories, you have taken an important step toward acknowledging the powerful emotional memories that can invade the present when you are least expecting them. Your ability to identify the old experiences will make it much easier for you to do the exercises in later chapters that are designed to help you loosen the power of those experiences.

Exercise 2: Sorting Out Goals and Ambitions

While the preceding exercise helped you understand how envy can stem from childhood experiences, it is also helpful to identify ambitions that were formed when you were young but that still hold power. Many of our aspirations are based on magical thinking, fantasies, and definitions of happiness that are presented to us through the media. When we were children, we were easily impressed and allowed fiction to shape our own beliefs and goals. As adults, we develop a more realistic and mature understanding of what is truly important to us. Your answers to the following questions may help you sort out the differences.

Complete the following phrases based on the way you remember thinking when you were younger.

1. When I was in middle school, I wanted (very much, somewhat, not at all) to...

   ■ be on a TV show or on the news.

   ■ be rich enough to buy anything I wanted.

   ■ be the person in charge.

   ■ have my own office and put my feet up on the desk.

   ■ have everyone admire me.

   ■ win or be on the team that wins a national trophy.

   ■ get a standing ovation from a large crowd.

- be as beautiful as a movie star.

- have the latest and best clothes, cars, and games.

Complete the following phrases based on the way you think now.

2. Now that I am an adult, it's (very much, somewhat, not at all) important to...

- be as healthy as I can be.

- make sure that the people I love have what they need to be safe and healthy.

- do the kind of work that I am best suited for.

- have financial security so that I don't have to worry about paying the rent.

- have opportunities to work out, play sports, and do the hobbies I love.

- have time to spend with my friends and family.

- be able to plan for vacations that will let me do things I don't ordinarily get to do.

- buy the clothes that look the best on me and are easy to take care of.

If you can't see the differences in priorities, try completing phrases from part 2 from the vantage point of your preadolescent self, and phrases from part 1 from your present perspective. Most people find that the things they learn to value have little to do with the things they coveted when they were young. And yet the beliefs that were formed during childhood continue to influence us. When a childhood ambition is sparked, we may momentarily revert to the things that we once believed would make us happy. Winning and fame may be prizes that children see on the media, but they rarely bring the long-term contentment that adults learn to cherish.

CHAPTER 7

Rejection

The need for group membership is hardwired in all of us and serves to ensure survival of the species. Human infants are helpless and depend completely on adults for survival. Even adults are programmed to live communally in order to survive. Perhaps that is why the experience of being rejected is one of the most unbearable triggers of emotional overreaction.

The Pain of Rejection

Most of us have experienced some form of rejection, whether it was a failed romance, soured friendship, failure to make a team, or loss of a job opportunity to someone else. You might agree with the saying that "rejection is painful" and remember having physical symptoms along with the disappointment. Research in brain functions actually confirms that the brain experiences social rejection in the same way that it processes physical pain. Drs. Naomi Eisenberger and Matthew Lieberman (2004) have shown that the receptors for rejection are strongly connected to the part of the brain that detects physical injury. These scientists speculate that pain teaches us to avoid making the same mistake twice. Just as we learn not to touch the hot stove once we've been burned, we are motivated by a painful rejection to do things differently in order to avoid further rejection.

Early Experiences with Rejection

All triggers activate belief systems that can serve as fuel for the fire or as a balm to help us calm down. For that reason, it is important for you to consider some of your early experiences with rejection. Experiences that were the most difficult, or that happened repeatedly, have the potential to be reactivated years later.

Peer Rejection

Many of us experience a form of rejection at school. Part of growing up is learning to function on our own without a parent or sibling to help us communicate our needs and work things out. For many of us, starting school was one of the earliest times when we were left on our own to deal with a large group of other children our own age. While many of us think of school as the place where we learned how to read and write, being at school taught us other lessons as well. School-age children learn how to make friends, how to stand up to the scrutiny of others, how to manage interpersonal conflict, and, all too often, how to deal with exclusion.

Social standing is very important to children as they learn to evaluate other children and recognize their own worth in the eyes of others. Even when children feel completely accepted by loving family members, they must learn to face the process of being scrutinized and judged by their peers. For most of us, this early school experience was the first time that personal differences were identified and brought to our attention. Suzy may never have thought twice about wearing her older sister's clothes until one of her classmates makes a joke about the way she looks in hand-me-downs. Robby may have adjusted easily to wearing eyeglasses like his parents and elder brothers and not understand being taunted by a class-mate who calls him "four eyes." But when Suzy and Robby realize that others are laughing at them or refusing to let them join their play group, they will have their first experience of shame and social rejection.

Childhood Shame

Being shamed by others is a particularly uncomfortable feeling. Years ago, psychoanalyst Eric Erikson (1950) recognized the psychological harm created by shame. In school, children judge others as being desirable or undesirable. The way that you handled this process when you were younger is likely tied to the level of self-esteem you possess now as an adult. Group acceptance and exclusion seem to peak in middle school, when preadolescent children are creating their identity beyond their family. Despite efforts to curb bullying, children are routinely victimized by classmates and often suffer lifelong emotional scars from it.

Just as children react to envy by either becoming aggressive or withdrawing, they react to social rejection with the same two major response patterns. In the face of rejection, a child might become enraged and turn aggressively against the child who is attempting to spurn her. She might also take out her anger on a different child or even reject someone else in order to make someone else the victim. A different child might react in an entirely different way and accept the rejection and humiliation, believing that he is worthless. Typically, that kind of child will withdraw and become very sad or even depressed. Both responses have the potential to become dangerous—to the child, as well as to others. Research on the students who commit or attempt school massacres shows that they have been socially rejected by others and made to feel shamed (Leary, Twenge, and Quinlivan 2006).

Carrying Shame into Adulthood

Dr. Brene Brown (2006) speaks of the intensely painful sense of being flawed and therefore unworthy of belonging. To Brown, the worst part of shame is the way it makes a person feel trapped and isolated, as if she is the only one who is different and unacceptable. Because of self-doubt and the sense of not fitting in, many women who have experienced rejection eventually turn to alcohol or drugs as a way to numb themselves from the excessive pain. For this reason, Brown believes that women who are substance abusers need to confront the vestiges of shame in order to get past the lingering emotions.

However, some adults try to resolve their emotional scars by taking the opposite position. In fact, some adults who experienced childhood shame are the ones you would least suspect of it. Children who have been emotionally injured need a parent who can comfort them. If they receive sufficient validation and soothing, they learn how to make themselves feel better when they're having a bad moment. However, if a child can't count on anyone to help him get through it, he might learn to undo the injury by taking a grandiose posture. Rather than suffer through an experience of being made to feel "less than," he decides to compete and excel in order to constantly prove to himself and others that he is "better than." While this reaction may seem like a reasonable solution, he will grow into an adult who must always compete in order to establish his superiority. Rather than soothing himself when there's a downturn, he must depend entirely on outside validation to help him remember his value. The remnants of shame and self-doubt can only be kept out of sight by the proof that comes with winning or reaching goals. Unfortunately, yesterday's victories don't last very long, and the push for renewed affirmation takes over.

Whatever path we take—succumbing to old wounds or fighting to stay away from them—unresolved childhood rejection makes us vulnerable to overreactions.

■ DANIEL'S STORY

Daniel told me that he often felt like the comedian Rodney Dangerfield, who typically ended his routine by saying, "I don't get no respect." Daniel knew that he had always been sensitive to feeling excluded but decided to start therapy after he had completely lost his temper at a professional organization in front of hundreds of his colleagues. The group had been meeting to discuss a new license and to create categories that would allow experienced members who had taken prior training to be exempt from the new exam. Things had gone smoothly until the group turned to the program that Daniel had taken. One board member felt that it was less thorough than the course of study he had taken and that graduates from that program should not be grandfathered in. Daniel had always disliked this man and considered him to be arrogant and self-serving.

But he surprised himself when he jumped up from his seat and started hurling personal insults at the man. Two friends rushed over and led him out of the room, but Daniel's behavior caused quite a stir.

In therapy, I asked Daniel to talk to me about times in his life that he had felt excluded or rejected. Daniel immediately spoke of his passion for basketball and how much he had loved shooting hoops in the neighborhood he grew up in. But as luck would have it, Daniel took after his mother's side of the family and by sixth grade was the smallest kid in the class. One of his worst childhood memories was the day he went to try out for the school basketball team and was not chosen. Even in gym class, students didn't seem to want him on their teams.

In time, this feeling of being "less than" grew even worse. Daniel felt that being short made it impossible to be socially accepted, as most of the girls he knew would only date guys who were taller than them. In Daniel's mind, the belief that people wouldn't think he was good enough carried over to other parts of his life. Daniel even thought that his parents showed more concern for his younger brother than for him. If his brother complained about something, then everyone seemed to fuss, but when Daniel got a bad break, people seemed to just shrug their shoulders. "It's only Daniel," he would imagine them saying.

Daniel remembered how quickly he had reacted at the professional meeting. When he experienced his colleague as trying to diminish Daniel's training, Daniel felt a surge of hatred. His heart started to pound and his face felt hot. In that moment, this man represented all the people who had tried to exclude him from things he knew he was able to do. In the face of rejection, Daniel just had to fight back.

Romantic Rejection

As much as it hurts to get a letter of rejection or be cut from a team, losing at love can be the most painful form of rejection of all. Being loved is the ultimate form of acceptance and is vital to our sense of connection and belonging. However, as most of us have discovered, finding and keeping love is complicated.

Unrequited Love

Therapists, philosophers, and poets have struggled to define what true love is. Research based on neurophysiology suggests that specific parts of the brain are activated through love. There is also research that shows how the brain responds to visual pleasure, smells that contribute to sexual attraction, and physical connection. While this helps to explain the chemistry that exists between two people, it does not completely explain what happens when a person falls in love.

Adolescents often refer to social ranking as they decide on potential dates. Anya would think twice about flirting with a high school senior if she was "only" a freshman. Paul would think twice about asking out a girl who was part of the "cool" crowd if he hung out with "techno-nerds," who mainly talked about computers and gaming. And yet we have all been influenced by fairy-tale romances in which the kissed frog turns into a prince and Cinderella's fairy godmother turns her into a dazzling beauty who captures the heart of the prince. Being chosen by someone special is a source of validation that becomes an opportunity to revisit perceived self-worth. But when someone rejects you as a romantic partner, there is a suggestion that you are not good enough in their eyes. Being made to feel less than or unworthy is a form of social rejection that actually stings. Once again, the part of the brain that processes social rejection contributes to the pain of unrequited love.

Rejection as Abandonment

Although being rejected is painful for everyone, there are certain people who are truly crushed when a romance ends. Their experience is not only about shame or not being good enough, but also about a dread of being alone. If you fit into this category, then rejection can feel like a catastrophe because it unleashes an unspoken fear of being vulnerable in a world that is not to be trusted.

Psychiatrists and mental health professionals believe that early childhood experiences prepare us for intimacy (J. P. Siegel 2000). A person who has a pattern of repeatedly searching for an ideal partner only to end up being quickly disappointed or rejected may be motivated by a fear of being alone. This problem typically develops when the person's parents were so self-absorbed or immersed in their own problems that they weren't available to soothe the child. In these kinds of families, tension and problems spread from family member to family member like one domino striking the next one in line. To make matters worse, these families tend to have reactions based on splitting, so that a small problem can quickly spiral into a crisis. As a result of being exposed to too much stress and too little soothing, the grown child continues to search for someone who can truly understand and be there as a loving and calming influence.

If this describes your situation, then you probably know that problems start because you want a relationship to work so badly that you overlook minor flaws and concerns. This is another form of splitting, as the red flags are overlooked in order to keep the perception of a "perfect" new friend or partner. In time, these issues create problems that prove to be unsolvable, but the truth is, those problems were there from the beginning.

■ ROSEMARY'S STORY

Rosemary originally came to therapy with Richard, her boyfriend of two years. She had given him an ultimatum to either propose or leave her alone, and he had suggested that they start therapy together. I was a little surprised when he asked if he could have a session alone with me, but Rosemary gave her consent and encouraged him to try to work on his reluctance to commit. However, when Richard met with me, he explained that he had told Rosemary from the beginning that he was not ready to marry, and that if he ever did marry, he would choose a woman who shared his religious background. He had enjoyed dating and traveling with Rosemary but had no intention of ever settling down with her. The reason he had come to therapy was to make sure that Rosemary was in good hands when he ended the relationship, because she had threatened suicide in the past when he had tried to end things.

Richard told Rosemary it was over a few days later, and Rosemary came to see me in a state of despair. She hadn't been able to sleep, eat, or work, and her eyes were so swollen from crying she could barely keep them open. After I was satisfied that Rosemary was not suicidal, we started to work on her grief and loss. Although it is appropriate to be deeply upset after a relationship ends, Rosemary's inability to focus on anything else was quite extreme. Even weeks later, when she was able to start working again, she would obsess over every word Richard had said, trying to look for clues that would convince her he was still available or that he had fallen for another woman but she could win him back. Rosemary's mind was constantly spinning, and over the next few weeks her image of Richard became increasingly one-sided. Her sense of his perfection as a boyfriend, lover, and potential husband persisted, despite information that she provided that showed how self-centered and manipulative he had been throughout their time together.

In therapy, I tried to help Rosemary make sense of her idealization of this young man. Rosemary came from a large family and had three elder brothers and a younger sister. Her father had died unexpectedly when Rosemary was eight, and the family lifestyle changed from working-class comfort to barely making ends meet. Rosemary had been her father's favorite child, and losing him had been unbearable to her. But for reasons that were hard to comprehend, Rosemary's mother grew angry and refused to let the children speak about the father who had abandoned them through death. Rosemary's life changed for the worse as her mother became increasingly withdrawn and exhausted. Although Rosemary had been a good student, she decided to leave home the day she graduated from high school, using her savings to become a calligrapher. She got an excellent job in an exclusive boutique and indulged herself with the latest fashions. Richard was attracted to her stylish beauty and playful nature and could afford to take her to the most expensive restaurants and clubs. He introduced her to a jet-set lifestyle and bought her jewelry and clothing that she couldn't afford on her salary.

Even though Richard had told her repeatedly that he wasn't interested in marriage, Rosemary preferred to keep her own secret fantasy about their future. She window-shopped for engagement rings, cut pictures of wedding dresses out of magazines, and even went through name books trying to imagine what to call their children. In many ways, Richard had become a father figure who would indulge and protect her for the rest of her life. Her fantasies had somehow become real to her, and she couldn't believe that Richard wouldn't be equally happy with the life she imagined. To keep this fantasy, Rosemary denied all of Richard's shortcomings. She knew that he had cheated on her multiple times during their relationship and lied to her about his family and job. Nonetheless, her wish to preserve her fantasy kept those events out of her mind. The man she grieved over was never real—he had been heavily embellished by her imagination. His rejection of her took her to a state of desperation where she imagined herself always on the outside of a life she yearned for. She started to see herself through Richard's eyes, as a woman from the wrong part of town with the wrong religion and no formal education. Without him, she was worthless, and his rejection proved that she wasn't good enough to be loved.

Rosemary's overreaction illustrates the importance of splitting, flooding, and denial. She had pushed aside important information throughout the relationship in order to see Richard and her future with him as perfect. Being with him also raised her self-esteem, but this ultimately contributed to the intensity of her pain when he ended the relationship. Finally, the emotional memories related to her lost father magnified the grief of losing a man who could pamper and protect her.

Tolerating Rejection

The emotional memories that are activated when we are rejected often go back to experiences in middle school and adolescence. When we were children, we allowed group dynamics to inform our ranking and social order. Being excluded meant that we didn't fit in with the kids with whom we wanted to associate. As adults we can try to acknowledge that not everyone gets along and that there are often reasons behind a rejection that we may never know. People can decide to end a relationship or choose to hire another person, but that decision should not determine our self-worth. Perhaps we believed that when we were young, but as we mature, we can choose to not give other people the power to decide whether or not we are good enough. As adults, we have a clearer sense of our real strengths and are no longer dependent on other people to shape our identity.

Processing the Feeling of Rejection

Belonging is a basic human need. Any rejection will create a sense of discomfort and pain, but that can be a momentary response. The deeper pain that rejection can stimulate comes from a belief that we are worthless or unlovable. Remember, the amygdala can make us experience emotional intensity that may be greater than the situation calls for. As we begin to connect our thoughts and feelings, the pain will subside. Consider these questions:

- Does this rejection really mean that you have nothing of value to offer?

- Do you know all the circumstances behind the decision of the person who rejected you?

- Are you flooding with emotional memories of other times you have lost something important?

- Is the feeling of being powerless to change this adding to your pain?

Reestablishing Perspective

Once we get past the emotional sting of being rejected, we can find ways to think about the real loss. The first thing is to reestablish your perspective. Consider these questions.

- Have you idealized the person or the gain that you were pursuing?

- Has this one incident made you believe that you will never get what you yearn for?

- Can you become more certain about what you truly want going forward?

- Can you imagine things you can do to make this dream come true?

Thoughtful Responses

In a thoughtful reaction, we are able to acknowledge the pain that comes with rejection. Loss is never easy, and it is important to be able to understand that something of value has been taken away. However, understanding the true value of the loss is crucial. In responding thoughtfully, we can ask ourselves if we have idealized the person, job, or opportunity and whether we now have the impulse to devalue it as a way of protecting ourselves from feeling more pain. We can also scan for emotional memories that are probably adding to the emotional experience. In the middle of an intense reaction, we need to focus on finding our way back to emotional equilibrium, but when we are calm again, there are important things to reflect on. Once we are certain that the old issues of self-esteem or shame that are related to childhood experiences have been defused, we can more honestly think about the lesson this rejection can teach us:

- If compatibility was an issue, did you have clues that were ignored along the way? How can this lack of compatibility sharpen your understanding of what you really want and what the other person in this situation was truly looking for?

- Are there things you should be changing if you want to pursue that kind of opportunity again?

- Is there any feedback that can be helpful as you decide the best way to move forward?

When we stop seeing rejection as an affirmation of worthlessness and start looking at the compatibility that is needed to make relationships with people or organizations flourish, we can learn much about what we really want in life. We also learn that, in many ways, we don't have the level of control that we wish we did—another important trigger that needs to be considered.

End-of-Chapter Exercises

Most people think that it is best to forget about incidents from the past that have created pain. However, if we allow these experiences to inform our self-image, then it is better to revisit these feelings than to try to forget them. The purpose of examining painful memories is to bring your adult perspective to situations that your childhood self had no way of challenging. If you find that the process is too uncomfortable, just jot down your thoughts and feelings in your notebook or journal and move on to the rest of this book. After you have read about the different ways to recover from extreme emotions in chapter 12, you can always return to this exercise and try again.

Exercise 1: Undo Childhood Shame

Try to remember a time when you were a school-age child and were excluded. There might have been a party that you weren't invited to, a team that you weren't chosen for, or a group that made it clear you weren't welcome to eat lunch at their table. Do you recall what was said or done to you that made you feel rejected?

Now bring your adult self to that situation. Try to imagine what weakness or insecurity led those children to be so cruel to you. Was it common for that group of children to exclude others? Do you think that any of those children may have experienced their own hidden doubts and insecurities?

We all have some parts of ourselves that we are uncertain about. By excluding others, children are trying to reassure themselves about their own self-doubts. Dominating others and establishing a pecking order may also have played a role in their acts of rejection.

Children also tend to make judgments based on differences—in appearance, cultural background, or athletic skill. Can you identify one thing about you that was different from the other children?

Now bring your adult self to that issue. Is it possible that something that once caused you to feel vulnerable when you were young ended up adding something unique and important to your life?

When we look at the differences that were the source of childhood shame from an adult perspective, we can often write a new script. Remember the story of the ugly duckling? Difference is not necessarily bad, even though it is an important aspect of why children reject one another. Think about other people you have discovered in your adult life who share and enjoy those things that made you "different" from other children. By embracing those parts of yourself, you are undoing emotional memories that have the power to make you reexperience unwarranted shame.

Exercise 2: Challenge Splitting

Taking the risk of wanting to be loved or chosen automatically raises the question "Am I good enough?" Too often we idealize a person or project and thereby give others too much power over determining our self-worth. Devaluing someone who has rejected you is not the answer and is just another signal that you are splitting. Think of a recent incident where you were rejected, then explore the following questions in your notebook or journal:

- Name three things that made this job or person attractive to you. What wonderful things did you dream might happen if this had worked out?

- Name three things that you weren't comfortable about. If these concerns or problems had gotten worse, what might have happened?

Remember, no one is perfect, but sometimes we want something so badly that we tune out or ignore the downside. If you had difficulty thinking of three things that were wonderful about that person or job, maybe that person or job isn't wonderful enough to warrant the intensity of your pain over the loss. But if you had difficulty coming up with three things that you weren't comfortable with, you are most likely idealizing the situation. Most things in life have pros and cons. When we see things as all good or all bad, we know that splitting has taken over.

CHAPTER 8

Criticism

While no one likes to be scrutinized and judged in an unfavorable way, the experience of being criticized can be a trigger that, for many people, unleashes extreme emotions. Consistently living up to expectations we have set for ourselves or that have been set by others seems almost impossible, and yet many people find it unbearable when they are told that they haven't done something well enough or need to do it in a different way. The rage, blame, and depression that can be produced by criticism rarely help resolve the situation. Often, the root of intense reactions to criticism is tied to narcissistic vulnerability.

Narcissistic Issues

When people hear the word "narcissistic," they usually think about someone they know who is stuck-up, selfish, arrogant, or all of the above. But when therapists think about narcissism, they look at it in an entirely different way; the narcissistic person isn't someone who has too much self-confidence but someone who has taken on a certain posture to protect herself from feeling "less than." Under the exterior of entitlement and superiority, there is a cavern full of self-doubt and fear of failing.

A child's need for approval and acceptance is fundamental to overall mental health. Whether it is the way parents react or the way a child interprets her parents' responses or a combination of both, a child who feels that she is only loved when she does things that please her parents will be at high risk for developing narcissistic vulnerability. If she grows up believing that when she does something well her parents are delighted, but when she fails to live up to their standards they will reject or humiliate her, then the seeds for splitting have been sown. Rather than learning to accept herself as an imperfect person who has both talents and shortcomings, she will strive to focus on only those parts of herself that had been good enough for others. Her shortcomings and other qualities that didn't earn the family's approval are pushed out of sight, and the memories of failing are filed into the "bad" drawer of her emotional filing cabinet.

There are several problems that are created by this solution. First, the child becomes dependent on other people to judge her self-worth. Just as she needs her parents to recognize and applaud her achievements in order to feel securely connected, she will go through life looking for other people to provide her with a sense of well-being rather than supplying that for herself. Second, even when she tries to ignore it, she senses that there are many aspects of herself that she must keep hidden. Rather than learn to judge for herself whether or not these traits are so terrible, she avoids acknowledging them. This leads to troubling feelings that include self-doubt, shame, and a sense of being a fraud. The effort it takes to keep these weaknesses concealed will make it intolerable for her to accept them in another person and resentful of the pressure to always be perfect. Third, if she ever gets criticized or fails to live up to her own standards, she is at risk for splitting and flooding, which create a downward spiral where the problem seems far worse than it really is. If weakness or failure opens the "bad" drawer of her emotional filing cabinet, she will be overwhelmed by the harshness of old emotional memories that compound how terrible it feels to fail. These dynamics put her at risk for being excessively critical of others and highly overreactive when someone criticizes her.

■ ADAM'S STORY

Adam had worked hard to build his company from the one-room office he had inherited from his father into a highly-respected firm with over eighty employees. He told his new hires that he demanded the best and that they would be rewarded for excellence. Adam liked to believe that he was a good mentor but had difficulty letting go of responsibility. He needed to review each proposal before it went out to make sure that it was thorough, accurate, and clear. If he found a flaw, he would simply correct it himself but hold the error as "strike one" against the employee. If something similar happened again, he would often erupt in a screaming tirade aimed at that employee and everyone associated with that project. Even after a few close associates commented to him that he was getting a pretty bad reputation, Adam clung to his right to demand perfection. He would occasionally try to make amends by joking and saying, "I don't say anything to another person that I don't say to myself," and decided that if people couldn't take the heat, they didn't fit into his company. One day, a business trip was unexpectedly canceled at the last moment, and he let himself in through the back entrance of his office suite. He was stunned and deeply upset to hear a group of his most trusted employees mocking his latest rage attack. They joked about his abysmal leadership skills and shared stories of errors that Adam had made that somehow were excused. Adam felt humiliated, betrayed, and overcome with a profound sense that their criticism was justified. It took days for him to shake the sense of shame and guilt he had for having become such a pathetic figurehead. What Adam had wanted the most was affirmation and respect; what he had earned was the opposite.

External Critics

Whether at work or in private life, there will always be people who judge us unfavorably. Sometimes we react as if a critic is intending to hurt us, and we become defensive or go on the attack. Our ability to distinguish the motives of those who criticize us is important but complicated.

Loaded Criticism

Often, criticism is loaded with forces that are intended to reduce you rather than help you. In chapter 6, I spoke about the sibling rivalry and childhood competition that come from the need to be recognized. The wish to be the best may begin in childhood, but it certainly doesn't end there. Just as the leader of an animal pack is the one who is able to demonstrate strength in order to dominate, certain people also strive to capture power by diminishing the competition. Working closely with others evokes the kind of competition that exists among siblings and can unleash aggressive envy if a coworker is promoted or recognized (Vecchio 2000, 2005). Criticism from a peer may reveal a layer of competition that you were formerly unaware of, providing you with important information about the system in which you are operating. There is a difference between honest feedback from a peer offered in a supportive way to help you improve or advance and comments that are intended to reduce you in the eyes of others.

Top-down criticism may also be more aggressive than is necessary. Drs. Jenny Hoobler and Daniel Brass confirmed a trickle-down pattern where recently criticized supervisors tended to pass that on to the people who reported to them. Even worse, supervisors who felt disenchanted with their company or thwarted in their personal progress were found to be hostile and even abusive toward employees who reported to them. Researchers also speculate that narcissistic employees may become aggressive when their performance evaluation isn't confirmed by senior management. Since they are not able to resolve problems with their own superiors, they act out against the people who are below them on the ladder (Hoobler and Brass 2006).

Loaded criticism may also be related to a larger problem within the company or system. There is a history of events that occurred before you came onto the scene, and that history may persist in spirit. If, through affiliation or personality, you come to represent one side of a former conflict, then you may receive residual disapproval or condemnation for a problem you had nothing to do with. This can occur in families as well as companies.

■ ELAINE AND JEFFREY'S STORY

Elaine and Jeffrey worked hard to make their marriage strong. It was a second marriage for both, and they realized how lucky they were to have found compatibility, humor, and shared values. Both felt very comfortable sharing their most honest feelings and thoughts, so Elaine was shocked when Jeffrey started to criticize her for being rigid and a fun killer. Jeffrey explained to me that he had a small extended family but had a few cousins who liked to spend time with him on the weekends. The couple had fought when Jeffrey accepted a cousin's invitation for the couple to spend a day at his beach home. Rather than be happy with this plan, Elaine had asked, "Why would you want us to spend a whole day with him? Didn't you tell me that he was being investigated for insurance fraud and hadn't paid any child support for two years?" Jeffrey had burst into a stream of criticism and complaints and accused Elaine of trying to prevent him from being close to anyone but her.

When I asked Elaine to talk about her comments, she explained that she had only met this cousin twice before and certainly didn't want to prevent Jeffrey from being close with any relative he wanted to. "But," she continued, "Jeffrey talks about this cousin quite a bit, and all I ever hear is the bad stuff. From what I hear, he is not exactly reputable. He certainly hasn't done the right thing with his children or his business. I'm only basing my opinion of him on what Jeffrey has told me."

As Elaine explained her perspective, Jeffrey could see how his comments had, in fact, been one-sided. He explained that the stories that had unfolded in the past year didn't undo the countless wonderful memories of the fun the two boys had shared growing up. While Jeffrey had a hard time figuring out what had led his cousin to do the things that he also disapproved of, his love for his cousin went back to the good times they had accumulated over the years.

Jeffrey's mother had been critical of his cousin and just about everyone on his dad's side of the family. She seemed to think her side of the family was better and sabotaged Jeffrey's plans to hang out with his father's brothers and their sons. This theme had been repeated in his first marriage, as his ex-wife had been critical of almost all of his friends The worst part was that both his mother and his ex-wife made it seem that if he didn't share their opinions, there was something wrong with him. Instead of wondering what Elaine was basing her comments on, Jeffrey had experienced her as being the same as two women from his past who had imposed their judgments on him for too long. Elaine had simply stepped into a loaded situation with little information to guide her.

Reenactments

Just as children repeat a theme in their play until it somehow no longer holds interest for them, adults tend to act out their predicaments with people who give them that opportunity. Self-esteem and self-confidence are tender aspects of well-being and can easily be damaged. People who feel diminished may try to reverse that feeling by viewing another person as the one who is diminished. By blaming or devaluing another person, they can feel better about themselves. They are reenacting a situation where someone is perceived as incompetent, but in this version, they get to play the opposite role.

Helpful Criticism

Although the word "criticism" has come to mean "judgment" and to imply failure, criticism is often offered as a way to make things better. Although it is true that being criticized means that you are being evaluated, the criticizer may be seeing you as part of a larger situation that needs to change.

Criticism as Feedback

Often, a comment that feels like criticism is actually a form of feedback, or information that helps a system regulate itself. A thermostat, for example, helps "inform" the furnace of the temperature of a dwelling. When the house has reached the desired temperature, the thermostat supplies feedback to the furnace so that the furnace can shut down at the appropriate time. When the house becomes cold again, the thermostat provides information so that the burner "knows" that it's time to kick in again. The thermostat is providing information that is vital to the successful work of the furnace. The thermostat isn't criticizing the furnace as being too strong or poor a performer but only providing the information that is required for appropriate cooling down or heating up.

This kind of information is particularly useful to have when we are working closely with others, whether that be at home or at work. It is also important to be receptive to feedback when we are trying to learn a new skill or take on new responsibilities. Simply deciding to do something doesn't make anyone an expert. There's always a learning curve, and starting out means starting at the bottom.

If you are the kind of person who bristles when anyone has a comment about your performance, you might ask yourself whether there's a discrepancy between the way you evaluate yourself versus the way others view you. If the criticism concerns an area you feel confident about and you have narcissistic tendencies, then you are quite likely to have an emotional overreaction. This was shown in an interesting research study in which subjects went through two related but different scenarios (Rhodewalt and Morf 1998). In the first part of the experiment, the subjects were given a task that was easy to perform correctly. They were asked to rate themselves and they received outside evaluation as well. Obviously, this part of the experiment was a win-win scenario. But in the second part of the experiment, the task was purposefully made impossible, and the subjects became extremely frustrated. Suddenly, they weren't able to get the results they had before or to live up to their own expectations. The combination of failure following success also made them more reactive to the evaluation of the external viewers. Subjects who had no expectations of how well they were going to do struggled with the difficult task but did not get upset with the outside evaluations.

In other words, if you see yourself as a beginner, you might be receptive to feedback that will help you improve. You expect to make errors, and you can forgive yourself when you make small mistakes. As you gain expertise, your evaluation of your progress in combination with the positive feedback from others makes you feel more secure and confident in your ability. These may be the situations for which it becomes most difficult to receive critical feedback. If the external review focuses on things you believe you can do well enough, the discrepancy in how you perceive yourself versus the way you are viewed by others may make it difficult not to feel bad.

Criticism as Useful New Information

In any situation that involves other people, there will always be a need for new information. Our worlds at home and at work are constantly changing, and we need to change along with them. Sometimes you may perceive a comment as unfair criticism when it is actually a request for change. The person providing the criticism is really asking you to comprehend that circumstances have changed and that he needs you to do something differently for his sake. In this kind of situation, you need to focus less on defending what you are used to doing and more on the end goal. If you ultimately want this relationship or situation to succeed, then the information you are hearing is truly an opportunity to make things better for everyone involved.

■ MELANIE'S STORY

Melanie thoroughly enjoyed being a mother. Even though there were days when her two daughters were at each other's throats or very demanding, she believed that she had raised daughters who possessed the values that were most important to her. Even though Brenda, the elder of the two, would be entering high school in two months, Melanie had confidence that Brenda would make healthy decisions and keep a good balance between schoolwork, sports, friends, and community volunteer work. She was thrown off guard when her younger child Julia, almost eleven at the time, responded sarcastically when Melanie asked her if she had put on sunscreen as they headed to her tennis lesson. While Melanie was accustomed to Brenda's tendency to want to do things for herself, this comment from Julia had a hostile flavor that Melanie wasn't used to. Melanie was even more shocked by what happened next. After she casually responded that she only had Julia's best interest at heart, Julia got even angrier: "Mom, you always need to be in control and make sure that everyone does things exactly the way you want. I'm getting sick of it."

Melanie felt like she was being kicked in the stomach. She felt a surge of anger and was tempted to tell Julia that she was an ungrateful brat. But while she was trying to compose herself and think of what to do, Brenda stepped in. "Mom, please don't get angry. Julia is trying to tell you something that I feel too sometimes. We know you only want the best for us, but if you constantly check up on us, then it makes us doubt that we can do the right thing all by ourselves. We're just not little kids anymore, and we don't like it when you treat us like we are." Melanie's anger turned into shame, but then she was able to think about how wise her daughters were. She looked at them with pride, recognizing that they really weren't little girls anymore. This conversation was exactly what she had needed to prepare herself for moving on to the next set of parenting challenges: providing her children with the space they needed to learn how to fly on their own. Chances are that Julia had put sunscreen on, and second-guessing her wasn't going to be helpful. Better to have a daughter with red cheeks than a daughter who has no self-confidence and needs to depend on other people to make decisions for her. Better yet is to have a daughter who believes in herself and knows how to stand up for herself in order to express her feelings and request change.

Internal Critics

People who work or live with individuals who are demanding know how relentless and critical they can be. What they don't understand is that the intolerance of failure isn't just reserved for others. People with narcissistic tendencies can be just as vicious to themselves when they don't perform well.

Children who grow up in homes where one or both parents were demanding and critical have a higher chance of developing a strong internal critic. Unlike others, who eventually make peace with their imperfections as long as the good qualities outweigh the bad, children from narcissistic families must be vigilant in guarding against the humiliation and rejection they believe their imperfections will evoke. I have worked with many people who only remember earning their parents' approval and love. At the same time, they can tell me about one or both parents displaying terrible tempers in dealings with other family members.

When a child unconsciously identifies with a parent, he takes on many qualities that in later years he might question or even regret. Even parents who offer love and security can at times be dominating and demanding. All these qualities will be absorbed into the developing child's sense of self, leading to an internal voice that mimics parental beliefs and expectations. If that critical, demanding voice is one that you are familiar with, then you may find that it has the power to induce unbearable disappointment and shame. Even a minor setback or failing can open the "bad" drawer of the emotional file cabinet and unleash extreme feelings of worthlessness and even self-loathing.

Creating Your Own Glass Ceiling

A demanding inner critic has the potential to help you set goals and work hard to reach them, but a punitive inner critic can have the opposite effect. Because even small failings can lead to splitting and episodes of depression and hopelessness, you might decide to give up altogether and not even try. Or you might create a glass ceiling so that you never have to face the test of your own potential—another common solution. People who compromise this way tend to use excuses and procrastination in order to create a lowered set of expectations. Rather than devote their full energy to a situation that may reveal them to be inadequate, they have a ready excuse if they don't quite perform up to par. Their goals are far less than their talents deserve, but the glass ceiling prevents them from having to face a punitive inner critic who can punish them if they should fail.

Being Overextended

In my private practice, I work with many couples who have become disenchanted and disconnected from each other. Often, one partner is trying to request that something very important be changed. Rather than hear that as new information, the other partner's response is frequently a defensive explanation or a protest against being criticized. It is not unusual for one partner to say, "I never hear about all the good things I do, just the one or two things that aren't exactly right." I have learned that this response really means, "I do so many things that are taken for granted and I get so little recognition or appreciation. I give so much more than I get back. And now you want even more."

This is as true in the work world as it is at home. Dr. Daniel Coleman (1998) notes the damage that comes with burnout, particularly when it is accompanied by isolation, unfairness, and skimpy rewards. Even without a challenging economy, building a successful career requires commitment and long hours. In an era of layoffs and cutbacks, things are even worse. Most employees are asked to take on more work with little or no additional compensation and no job security. The result is a high level of burnout and disenchantment, which can breed cynicism and emotional withdrawal at work and at home.

Time away from work used to present opportunities to replenish and renew, but a new set of standards and expectations has been created there as well. Working parents struggle to meet the demands of children, work, maintaining a home, relationships with extended family, and marriage. Parents also find that the time they assume is theirs for relaxation or personal interests is actually consumed with responsibilities that must be shared to keep home life in order, making for child-centered and schedule-dominated families. The result is that adults are overburdened and emotionally undernourished.

If you have allowed yourself to fall into this cycle of endless giving, then you will have little tolerance for any complaint. In truth, you have given more than you should be expected to give, and at enormous cost to your own well-being. If you are operating from an overextended position, then what you need the most is to have someone acknowledge your efforts and give you opportunities to restore your strength. Chances are that you will automatically resent anyone who seems to be placing additional burdens on you or who devalues what you have produced at enormous effort.

Many of us have set standards for ourselves that are exceedingly high. At the same time, we view asking for help as a sign of weakness or incompetence. If we find ourselves in an ongoing situation in which there are multiple demands and few resources, we will eventually become depleted. In the absence of balance and nourishment, any criticism can seem unreasonable and cruel. The trick is to identify these trends so that you can prevent the circumstances before they lead to the perfect storm.

Tolerating Criticism

Criticism has the power to activate intense and uncomfortable feelings. When we are criticized, we may feel vulnerable, exposed, unfairly picked on, exploited, put down, humiliated, or rejected. Criticism can create anxiety by challenging our security, our right to belong, our sense of self-worth, and our self-image. As in any situation that involves group and family membership, the threat to our well-being will be perceived by our amygdala as an immediate danger. Sometimes the instinct to detect danger is actually justified if the person who has criticized us is not acting in our best interest. More often, we are being offered important information that provides us with useful feedback about the system we are a part of or a request for change that it's in our interest to acknowledge. To sort it all out, we need to check our urge to react until we can get grounded and respond thoughtfully.

Oversensitivity

As much as you may find this difficult to acknowledge, it is important to know if you are predisposed to oversensitivity to any criticism. Ask yourself these questions:

- Does any kind of negative appraisal tend to put you in a bad mood?

- If you can't learn a sport or hobby quickly, do you tend to just quit?

- Do you find yourself making excuses so that people won't think badly of you?

- When someone criticizes you, is your first thought to blame someone else?

- Did you grow up with a sibling or parent who was put down for weaknesses?

- Are you too focused on what other people think of you?

- Do people tell you that you are too sensitive?

- Do you tend to beat yourself up whenever you make a mistake?

- Do you ruminate and have a hard time letting go of situations in which you were critiqued?

- Do you tend to procrastinate or set up excuses so that no one expects too much of you?

- Do you secretly think that you are smarter or better than most of the people you interact with?

If you answered yes to most of these questions, your inner critic has taken too much power over your life. As a child, you learned about standards by living in a world that was created by adults. As an adult, you have the option of deciding for yourself whether the dance of perfection is worth all the angst and pain it is costing you. Chances are that even a small failure can push you into the "all bad" emotional drawer, and your efforts to ward off the damage that criticism wreaks prevent you from getting the benefits that new information can provide.

Processing Criticism

Although there is an initial sting whenever you hear something about yourself that isn't positive, it is important to sort through the defenses and emotional memories that may be adding to your level of discomfort. Splitting and flooding can make you generalize and exaggerate so that a simple failure is no longer about one incident but about you as a person. If one incident, evaluation, or comment has the power to put you in the "all bad" drawer, then you need to identify the generalizations that are likely adding insult to injury. Ask yourself the following questions.

- Is this feedback about one thing you do that isn't working for others or about everything you do in that role?

- Is this person asking that you change in order to fit in better, or are you inferring from what was said that you will be removed or replaced?

- Do you really believe that you are so perfect that you never make mistakes? If you can admit to messing up on the problem that was brought to your attention, does it mean that you have no value at all?

- Are you so focused on explaining or justifying the past that you cannot imagine how to use this information as feedback that can make things better in the future?

If you are overly focused on explaining the past, you will not be able to see how much better things could be going forward. If you are mainly concerned with locating fault, then it will be impossible for you to comprehend the lesson that could help improve your life (Stucke and Sporer 2002).

Thoughtful Responses

A thoughtful response to criticism begins with acknowledging the nature of emotional discomfort that it has stimulated. You identify feelings that have erupted in order to help you sort through the different components of this experience. If you know that you have a tendency to be too harsh with yourself or if you are fatigued or emotionally depleted, you can remind yourself that seeing the positive will be challenging but is ultimately more important than trying to defend yourself.

To put the criticism into context, take a moment to consider the source. Is the person offering criticism someone you trust and who typically wants you to succeed? If so, is this an attempt to offer you valuable information? If the message seems negatively charged, is it possible that the delivery has more to do with circumstances that extend beyond the two of you? Is something about the way the message is being delivered making it difficult to focus just on the information?

If this person is not someone you know well, or is someone you have no reason to trust, ask yourself if this exchange is a form of anger or domination. Is this someone who views herself as competing with you in some way? Is this person closely aligned with a subgroup that you have not been able to join? Does your status or recognition of you by a third party create envy or a threat to someone else that you might not have been aware of? If your amygdala has signaled danger, ask yourself if there may be more going on behind the scenes than you are aware of.

Most criticism contains important information. A thoughtful response allows us to look at the feedback and new information in ways that might actually help us to do a better job. If we respect that the source of the criticism has valid experience and is invested in making things work out, then our ability to absorb the useful part of criticism will make it easier to shift our perspective away from shame and blame.

End-of-Chapter Exercises

Most people tend to believe that the way they have handled situations in the past is due to inherent personality. Instead of viewing behavior as something they could change, they assume that the way they have responded in the past is the way they will continue to respond in the future. However, many of the ways that we learned to deal with criticism are related to experiences we had while growing up. The following exercises can help you look at patterns you might have learned when you were too young to know that there were alternatives.

Exercise 1: Challenging Splitting

In your notebook or journal, write down your answers to the following questions. Take as long as you need and use as much paper as you require.

Part 1

The parts of myself that I am most proud of are:

The parts that I like least about myself are:

Count up the number of virtues and flaws that you wrote down. Look at the ratio of good to bad. If your ratio was close to 50:50 or 60:40, then you seem to be comfortable with accepting both your assets and your limitations. If your ratio for good to bad is closer to 20:80, then you are viewing yourself through the eyes of a punitive inner critic. You have given in to a worldview and expectations for yourself that were created when you were too little to understand what was being asked of you. Your preoccupation with fault may lead you to become self-doubting and unable to stick with opportunities to reach positive goals. If you were only comfortable writing about your strengths and your ratio is 80:20, then you are under a lot of pressure to live up to high standards. You have difficulty tolerating weakness in yourself and others and may be so uncomfortable with your faults that it's hard to focus on improving them.

Part 2

Learning to forgive weakness in others is an important step.

First consider the traits or weaknesses you like the least in yourself. Write down one characteristic that you are ashamed of. Do you think one or both of your parents had a problem with this characteristic of yours? If so, think of a memory that made you come to that conclusion. What made it difficult for them to lighten up? Did either of your parents also have that characteristic that was judged so harshly in you? Were your parents able to forgive weakness in their children and other people, or did they tend to hold on to minor transgressions?

Now focus on yourself. How easily do you forgive others who have let you down? How easily do you forgive yourself for the weaknesses you just wrote about? Often our push for perfection and our difficulty accepting weakness in ourselves and others is absorbed along with other family values that were modeled by our parents. We may never challenge this pattern or know that it is possible to choose a different option. If difficulty forgiving transgressions is a family pattern, then it's time to evaluate if it is a strength that brings happiness and success or, in itself, a weakness that should be corrected. Challenging the past will be explored in more depth in chapter 13.

Exercise 2: Acknowledging Unmet Needs

Write down your answers to the following questions in your notebook or journal. Once again, take as much time and paper as you need.

- What are the challenges, pressures, and responsibilities in your life right now? How many hours are you working or worrying about these responsibilities?

- What are the things in your life that make you laugh or feel restored? How many hours a week do you get to do these things?

Look at the ratio of your challenges to the opportunities you have to replenish yourself. Do you think that you give yourself enough time to build the restorative energy required to balance your burdens? If not, answer the following questions:

- Is there anyone who could help share some of the load if you asked them?

- Do you have an opportunity to delegate but find that difficult to do?

- Do you tend to do for others without asking them to take over responsibilities they are capable of?

- Do you find it difficult to put your needs ahead of the needs of others?

- Do you find that you have said yes to too many commitments but can't back out?

- Does asking others for help make you uncomfortable? If so, think about reasons that might be behind your self-sufficiency:

  - You don't want to owe anything to anybody.

  - You don't want others to see you as being inadequate.

- You couldn't stand being turned down, so it's better not to ask.

- You just don't believe that the people in your world would do much for you.

- You value your ability to live up to your responsibilities.

- You have never taken the easy way out and don't intend to start now.

- If people really cared about you, they wouldn't need to be asked to help.

- You just have a hard time asking for help.

Your emotional health can't fully recover unless you learn that it's okay to request help and to reconfigure the ratio of obligation to restoration so that you are not operating out of exhaustion. When you are emotionally or physically depleted, it will be almost impossible for you to hear a request for change as anything other than harsh criticism. Remember, some of the criticism that is difficult to hear is being offered as a form of feedback that could lead to improvement. When you are operating from a balanced posture, you can be more able to hear and respond to it that way.

CHAPTER 9

Control

Even though we live in a technologically sophisticated world, our emotional response system was created eons ago. We are primed to react intensely and immediately to perceived danger, which includes threats to our emotional security as well as to our physical safety. We are also hardwired to compete in order to establish our relative social status. These forces complicate our lives because we depend on group membership for survival, but we fight each other to get and keep what is best for us as individuals.

Personal Control

There is a difference between having control over ourselves and needing to be in control of others. However, the two positions can overlap when the things that we want involve making others participate or comply, or when others make demands on us that we're not comfortable with. Having control usually means having the power to allocate resources and determine outcomes. Often that means having the freedom to get what we want and protect the things that matter to us. While it is not possible to always get our way, we each have aspects of our lives that are central to our sense of safety and well-being. When we are unable to preserve control over these areas, we can stumble into feelings of helplessness and depression. In extreme situations, a lack of control can even strip us of the will to live.. With stakes that high, it is no wonder that even a relatively minor loss of control can evoke an intense emotional response.

Efficacy

The way that we assess our own abilities may be just as important as what we are able to actually do. Dr. Alfred Bandura (1997) uses the term "efficacy" to describe the way we judge our abilities. When we believe that we are capable of succeeding at a task, we become motivated and find ways to take action. Usually this entails taking control in order to reach our goal and making sure that nothing interferes with or prevents our doing so.

When we are confident that we will succeed, we may take risks and aggressively push through doubt. When we are fearful that we might fail, we tend to hold back from taking the lead. We allow others who possess more self-confidence or stronger efficacy to take risks that make us uncomfortable. Perhaps you can remember times in your school days when you knew the answer to a teacher's questions and enthusiastically waved your arm hoping to get picked. There were probably also times that you weren't so sure and timidly waited for someone else to speak up.

Our brain chemistry is different in times of certainty than it is in times of doubt. Some people just seem more extroverted and assertive, while others get anxious at the thought of being held responsible (Depue and Collins 1999; Haas et al. 2007). Either stance can activate the amygdala and set the stage for overreaction.

Overreactions may also be triggered when we believe that no one is in control. In the face of chaos, most people focus on the possible danger and become anxious. The phrase "out of control" suggests that there is the potential for disaster, and our amygdala prepares us to fight or flee. In this way, confidence propels us to seek control, self-doubt leads us to defer control to others, and a perception that no one is in control can create a sense of panic. The parts of the brain that monitor self-awareness also allow us to register the responses of those around us. Taking control or worrying about our capabilities makes it more difficult to stay attuned to other people who are involved in the situation.

■ ALEX'S STORY

Before the economy took a turn for the worse, Alex had felt confident and secure in his job. He had found the marketing job he wanted within months of graduating from college and had received two important promotions in the ten years he had been with the company. But last week he and the other directors were told that all divisions would have to face downsizing and cost-cutting measures that were necessary for the company to survive.

While Alex was comfortable taking a leadership role with the people on his team, he tended to offer few remarks at the senior management meetings. Although he had plenty of ideas, he wasn't comfortable arguing for something unless he was positive that it was the best solution. There were always two or three colleagues who jumped to express strong opinions that seemed rushed and half-baked. Usually, there were others who presented positions that were acceptable to him, or there was time for him to present a more thorough response in a follow-up meeting. But in a climate of downsizing, the nature of the decisions under discussion seemed to make everyone argue to protect their own best interests. In the face of the aggressive bantering, Alex found himself slipping into a silent, pessimistic mood.

In therapy, I asked Alex to describe the thoughts and emotions he experienced in that meeting. To prevent him from censoring himself, I asked him to exaggerate so that we could more easily explore possible connections. Alex surprised himself by describing a fear of hurting others or of doing something that couldn't be reversed. When I asked him to recall any other times in his life that he had felt like that, he recalled an incident that had occurred when he was in middle school.

He had been part of a group that disliked one kid who was always trying to tag along with them. One day he did something that ended up humiliating this kid in public. Instead of having his friends join in the laughing and ridicule, there was silence because the incident had been observed by a teacher who immediately sent Alex to the principal's office. Although the lecture and string of detentions was hard to face, the response from his parents was even worse. His mother had called him a bully and set up a meeting for the two families so that Alex could apologize to the boy and his parents. She also made him go to church with her for the next two months. His father said that he had never imagined that he would be this disappointed by his son and took away his bike-riding privileges.

Alex felt that the degree of humiliation and shame he had been made to feel was far worse than anything he had done to the kid he had embarrassed. He had learned that others could get away with aggressive behavior but that he would be the one who was caught and condemned for it. He also learned how quickly positions were reversed and how one act made from a position of security could quickly spiral into humiliation and shame. Although Alex had not thought about this incident for years, the statements he wanted to make in the management meetings would have been self-serving and competitive. Because that would be a public act that could potentially harm other members of a small group, his mind had made an unconscious link to the past and to the humiliation and loss of stature he had endured so many years ago. This perceived danger had created profound anxiety that led him to shut down—an immediate protective response that puzzled everyone, including Alex himself.

While explosions are more noticeable and tend to create more immediate harm, implosions can create different kinds of problems. If you find yourself becoming detached or tuning out, there may be an important issue that has made you feel overwhelmed because you do not feel in control or do not want to be put in a position where you have to take control. Your reason may be different from Alex's but may also have its roots in something that has little bearing on the situation at hand.

Learned Helplessness

In the mid-1960s, Drs. Martin Seligman and Steven Maier conducted a series of experiments in their laboratories at the University of

Pennsylvania (Seligman 1975). They were interested in learning how animals handle situations they have no control over. In their most famous experiment, dogs were given random electric shocks. In earlier experiments, the dogs had learned to stop the shocks by performing specific acts, but nothing they did worked in this experiment. Ultimately, the dogs gave up trying to control their situation and became subdued. They lost their interest in food, sex, and play and showed every symptom of being seriously depressed. Subsequent experiments with rats found that even when circumstances were changed so that the animals could later escape from the source of their distress, they had no motivation to even try. Drs. Seligman and Maier coined the term "learned helplessness" to describe a depression that is created when people conclude that they have no control over an ongoing, painful situation. In a state of learned helplessness, the future becomes bleak and a person stops caring.

When the theories of efficacy and learned helplessness are put together, you can see how important it is to believe that you are capable of doing things that will help you reach your goals. Believing in yourself promotes initiative and creates energy that pushes you toward action. Self-confidence helps you establish the expectation that you can control the outcome and succeed. In contrast, when you surrender control, you take a passive stance and rely on the strength and capabilities of others. And if you find that you have lost all control and have no power to influence what is happening, you may become enraged or could ultimately give up altogether.

Sharing Control

In a world of specialized knowledge and large organizations, we all encounter situations where we have little or no personal power. When we have absolute confidence that we are in good hands, surrendering control can be relatively easy. But if you are a person who has difficulty letting others take over, your life is probably much more stressful than it needs to be. You may also find that you avoid situations that put you in a passive position, even when avoiding those situations could be dangerous to your health.

Anxiety is an emotional response to perceived danger, but taking control is only one way to combat that anxiety. When you allow yourself to challenge the assumptions that create the anxiety in the first place, you will find yourself more comfortable relaxing in situations where you need to relinquish control. Often a sense of safety can be restored by knowing how things are going to unfold and by developing confidence in the people who will be in charge. For example, health care professionals have learned that patient education is an important way to promote compliance. By taking the time to explain a diagnostic procedure or treatment plan, they enable patients to more easily follow their instructions. We may not like having a medical procedure that requires us to stay perfectly still in an enclosed chamber while being exposed to loud noises, but our anxiety will diminish if we understand that it will only be for twenty minutes and that there will be short periods of rest between the times we need to stay still. Knowing what is going to happen next reduces the sense of helplessness and apprehension that is generated when we have no control over a situation.

Developing Control

As much as children enjoy the security and sense of safety that comes when parents rule, eventually they want to have more control over decisions that affect them. Even infants know when they want to get picked up or fed and are equipped with strong vocal skills that help them influence their environment. Getting what they think they need when they want it becomes a major theme of the "terrible twos," and children will have temper tantrums and screaming fits to make those in control bend to their wishes. Freud described this behavior as the pleasure principle and thought that regardless of education and socialization, people are born with an animal instinct to pursue pleasure. When we are intent on getting the things we want, we become aggressive in order to control the outcome.

Family therapists are trained to examine the power structure of the families they work with. Although different family structures exist in various cultures, in almost all families adults should be comfortable having authority over young children. For example, parents of young children should be comfortable with their power to take control by making and enforcing rules. That may sound obvious, but you might be surprised to find out that many parents can't do this and are actually ruled by their children.

Consequences of Taking Control

As children mature, they work to convince their parents that they are mature enough to make important decisions or at least to have a voice in how they want things to turn out. They soon learn that being responsible for their own decisions comes with a price tag of having to suffer the consequences when things don't work out. A boy who allows his parent to decide that he should go to basketball camp instead of computer camp can complain and criticize the parent if he doesn't end up liking it. But if he was the one who chose basketball camp, then he has only himself to blame—particularly if his parents didn't think it was such a good idea in the first place.

When parents fail to let older children make decisions and learn from their mistakes, things usually don't work out well in the long run. Parents who think they know best are often basing their opinions on their own preferences or on a vision of the way they would like their children to turn out. Difficulty acknowledging that their child is different from them prevents them from really enjoying the novel and unique things she can bring to their lives. If she is made to feel wrong or inadequate for not sharing her parents' dreams and goals, than she can either reject her parents altogether (perhaps turning to people outside of the family who seem more compatible) or sacrifice her own identity in order to comply with her parents' rigid expectations. Years later, she will continue to be reactive to others who criticize her or ask her to compromise. Despite her wish for personal control, she might even find herself pursuing strong people who seem confident about what is right and wrong.

Competing for Control

Part of becoming an adult is celebrating that you are finally old enough to make your own decisions. Getting your driver's license acknowledges that you are competent to drive and control a vehicle; being old enough to purchase alcohol means that you can be trusted with responsible decisions regarding your own health and well-being. Being old enough to vote doesn't put you in charge of running the country, but it does allow you to take some control through voting for the candidate you would like to have represent you. At the same time, becoming an adult brings us to the life stage where we are ready to form an intimate bond with another adult. Unfortunately, there are no two people who see things completely the same way, and control once again becomes a major issue.

When two individuals become a couple, they soon learn that what each one does has a huge effect on the other. Couples are faced with countless decisions, such as who takes over certain chores; whether they spend time with friends, family, each other, or alone; how they spend or save money; and how to furnish a shared space that incorporates two sets of preferences. Even when we feel compatible and committed to our partner, a request to compromise on something important can lead to conflict. In these situations, having control means having the final say.

Taking control in a relationship can be done in ways that are far from obvious and not always aboveboard. The power equation between partners does not have to be balanced all the time, as long as both agree to the trade-offs. Some couples believe that one spouse has more experience or capabilities in a certain area and should have greater power in those areas. However, when one partner tries to seize control, there are always complications. People learn to dominate in a variety of ways. Some people become assertive and threaten harm or adverse consequences. However, there are also subversive tactics that are equally unfair. A husband might try to discredit his wife or threaten to withdraw love or favors in order to get his way. A wife might try to prevail by bringing in outsiders who can weigh things in her favor.

The problem with all of these tactics is that relationships work best when there is a sense of trust and mutuality. We are more willing to sacrifice and compromise when we believe that our partner will do the same for us on a different occasion. Seizing what you want by force or questionable tactics erodes goodwill and leads partners to become suspicious, mistrustful, and adversarial.

From my vantage point, I see that this is a self-sabotaging cycle. Relationships thrive on the security that comes with commitment and caring. For example, if Peter gets upset because his girlfriend spends too much time on the telephone with friends, he may feel threatened, insecure, jealous, or deprived. His needs, in this case for companionship and validation, aren't being met, and he is being ignored while other people are getting the attention he wants. Peter can either trust that his partner will respond to his needs if he tells her how he is feeling, or decide that he has to take control of the situation and solve it by himself. If he uses power tactics to stop the phone calls, then his girlfriend will most likely feel resentful and angry. She might fight back or she might even decide to spend more time with her girlfriends out of spite or out of a need for sympathy created by Peter's harsh treatment. The only certain outcome is that by trying to seize control, Peter ensures that he will never get what he really wants.

Relinquishing Control

While it is important to understand the motives that propel some of us to take control, it is just as important to understand why others seem to defer or easily relinquish the control they could keep.

Fear of Conflict

Often, a fear of conflict leads us to give up too easily. Going against the wishes of a stronger person can be very unsettling for many of us and impossible under certain circumstances.

Children are easily frightened and made anxious by adult anger. Too many people were brought up in homes where they were exposed to family violence and have painful, emotionally charged memories of parents ridiculing, threatening, insulting, and even assaulting each other. When we witness or experience family abuse, the horror and fear is burned into our emotional memory banks. Even if we can't remember the details, the feelings can quickly be evoked in situations that hint at the potential for violence. Once the brain has developed a neural connection between disagreement and violence, the amygdala immediately perceives danger in disagreement and responds. Avoiding conflict may become the adaptive or at least the preferred option.

Fear of Abandonment

Parents who established control by withdrawing love and approval can also create problems for their children. Security is perhaps the most important childhood need and is built from the expectation that our parents will always be there to help us when we need it. When parents can't be trusted to provide comfort and reassurance, we have difficulty knowing whether it's better to keep trying to depend on them or whether we should give up. Some children handle this by clinging to their parents in order to get the reassurance they need, but others just seem to turn their backs and have difficulty trusting that anyone will ever be there for them. Years later, if your partner threatens to walk out because you are challenging his right to control the situation, then the old emotional memory of being abandoned may prevent you from risking any additional conflict.

Entitlement

Getting what you need can be even more complicated when you think you always deserve preferential treatment and the best of everything. *Entitlement* is a belief that your capabilities are superior to those of others and that certain privileges and exceptions should be granted to you. Frequently, entitlement goes hand in hand with narcissistic tendencies. Narcissism can be described as a pattern of defenses that makes people excessively dependent on feedback in order to regulate their self-esteem. The difficulty in tolerating weakness leads to the tendency to see things as being all or nothing, which is the hallmark of splitting (J. P. Siegel 1992). Under the influence of narcissism, we may become focused on the importance of our own needs and less able to see how that affects others (Judge, LePine, and Rich 2006). We might also lose the big-picture perspective and concentrate more on our need to prevail. When self-esteem is threatened, an overreaction is sure to follow.

Finding a Comfortable Balance

Finding a comfort zone with control is never easy. It requires that we have realistic confidence in our capabilities but can respect that others are competent as well, even when they have different ideas or goals.

Relinquishing control requires that we trust the people or organizations we have joined and accept that we won't always be able to influence the outcome of everything that is important to us. Being comfortable with loosening our grip often means asking others for help and acknowledging a dependency instead of just operating as if we can get everything we need by ourselves. It also means being able to risk conflict, which could occur when competing interests arise, and establishing our own value with the expectation that power and control can be shared. Problems with control almost always involve the despair that comes from having too little control or the antagonism that develops when we aren't comfortable sharing control with others.

Too Little Control

When we feel that we have no control, we are susceptible to learned helplessness and depression. The more we dwell on the things that seem out of control, the more helpless we become. Fighting to keep or take back control is only possible if you understand the beliefs that are holding you back. Consider these questions:

- What is being asked of you that you are afraid of?

- Do you doubt your ability to know what is best for yourself? If so, have you ever taken the lead in a similar situation and done it well? Why is this time different?

- Who stands to gain if you stay in a passive position?

- What is the worst thing that could happen if you decide to take a stronger stance?

- Are you afraid that this will lead to conflict?

- Are you afraid you will be rejected if you don't give in?

- Does standing up for yourself turn you into someone you despise?

Too Much Control

When we fight to take control, we are often being ruled by irrational anxiety or narcissistic defenses. Our need to make things happen exactly the way we envision shows that we haven't been able to trust that different ideas and approaches can improve our lives. Instead of justifying why your way is always better, consider these questions:

- Are you assuming that you always know what is best for yourself and everyone else?

- Are you worried about losing your power if you allow yourself to include others in the decision-making process?

- Will you lose or gain respect by allowing others to take a more active part?

- What's the worst thing that could happen if you trust someone to do something you think is important?

- Do you always have to count on yourself to get what you need?

- Are you setting yourself up for disappointment and heartache if you let yourself need something that has to be offered or volunteered?

- What are you missing by not letting anyone get close enough that you can depend on them?

Managing our need to take control is a two-edged sword. When we overreact to a threatening situation and get into full survival-tactics mode, our intensity and aggression hurt those we care about. When we allow self-doubt to rouse our anxiety, we abdicate control and become too dependent on others to take over for us. When we believe that we have no control over a difficult situation, we may give up altogether and become depressed.

A Thoughtful Response

In a thoughtful approach, we are able to acknowledge the aggression or anxiety that has been stimulated. Once you regain your equilibrium, take a closer look at the goal you were pursuing in order to understand its importance. Take time to acknowledge if your feelings were sparked by interrupted efficacy or a challenge to personal freedom, or if you are facing a situation that has raised self-doubt or helplessness. Ask yourself if your perception of the event has been clouded by splitting or entitlement and whether you are afraid to engage in a potential conflict over control. Only when you are sure that your interpretation of events is truly based in the moment can you judge the course of action that is in your best interest.

End-of-Chapter Exercise: Challenging Entitlement

The need to come out ahead is often fueled by narcissistic tendencies. In your journal or notebook, rate how often you think in the following ways in your relationships at work and home.

At work, I (always, sometimes, rarely)…

- am uncomfortable when others are recognized or promoted.

- have high expectations of people who report to me.

- tend to judge people quickly.

- do best with a hand-picked team.

- can't stand incompetence.

- am more comfortable giving than taking orders.

- am confident in my decision making.

- would rather stand alone than be grouped with people who are inferior.

- believe second-place isn't good enough.

- believe competition weeds out those who don't belong.

If you answered "always" to most of these questions, it's time to take a hard look at the way you interact with others on the job. When we think that we are smarter and more capable than those around us, we end up acting in ways that are dismissive and disrespectful. Organizations thrive on group cohesion and tend not to condone arrogant or exploitative behavior. Taking control in order to meet your own goals may feel like the most comfortable way of operating at work, but it will lead to interpersonal problems and errors that could easily have been prevented.

At home, I (always, sometimes, rarely)…

- think I am the force that gets the important things done in my family.

- believe if people followed my instructions, things would work out much better.

- can come up with a solution to any problem.

- have a strong will.

- know what's best.

- have high expectations for myself.

- can charm or influence others to go my way.

- find it difficult to compromise.

- have no empathy for people who make excuses.

If you answered "always" to most of these questions, take a moment to consider how these traits may be causing resentment and conflict in your family relationships. You may know what works best for you, but the people you love are just as unique as you are. Allowing others to be different may seem like a forced compromise at first, but it will bring tremendous rewards and enrich your life. Best of all, the climate in your home will relax as people start working in a more collaborative fashion.

SECTION 3

The Context

It is impossible to list every event or situation that might cause you to overreact. As much as we share genetic wiring that programs us to perceive and react to danger, the specific events that trigger *you* to overreact incorporate the emotional memories, schemas, and sensitivities that are unique to you. The mix of genetic, family, cultural, and environmental factors that shaped your personality and beliefs is one of a kind.

In chapters 10 and 11, you will be introduced to the stories of people who have been put in difficult positions at work and at home. If you find yourself identifying with their situations, response patterns, or underlying beliefs, take a moment to make a note of it in your journal or notebook. Often we learn about ourselves by understanding how things work for others. There are no exercises at the ends of these chapters. As a general practice, keep your notebook handy as you read these chapters and think about your own experiences at work and home. If you encounter a story or situation that you relate to, write down the themes and feelings you have experienced.

CHAPTER 10

Challenges at Work

Although most of us would like to believe that work is about logic and performance, there are a host of potential triggers that can cause us to emotionally unravel in that environment. Envy, rejection, criticism, and loss of control are powerful triggers and exist in almost all work situations. Even though the context may be completely different, the schemas and emotional memories that were created in the context of family and school are frequently and easily revived. Whether you implode or explode, an emotional overreaction can compromise your job performance and affect important relationships. Until you understand the triggers and beliefs that work behind the scenes, it will be difficult to manage reactions and decisions in a way that supports your success and well-being.

Costly Explosions

While not everyone reacts to stressful situations by getting enraged, most of us have lost our temper at one time or another. Every company or work setting has its own culture and informal rules about proper conduct, but many workplaces will not tolerate an employee who treats another employee or client with disrespect. An emotional explosion at work can be extremely costly to your reputation and credibility. In certain environments, it can even lead to termination.

■ PAUL'S STORY

Paul described himself as a perfectionist, but his high expectations often got in his way. Despite graduating medical school with top grades, he had floundered in his residency program and been forced to accept a position in a teaching hospital that he felt was beneath him. He didn't mind the interns that had been assigned to him but felt that the nursing staff was of a lower quality than the competent, self-assured professionals he had been exposed to during his medical training. The one who really annoyed him was Samantha, a soft-spoken woman who had worked at the hospital for almost forty years. While most of the staff seemed to value her experience and calm demeanor, Paul found himself constantly irritated by how slowly she walked and responded to questions. One day, Paul asked Samantha to retrieve a chart that he believed he had left on the rack outside a patient's room. Within minutes, Paul started to tap his foot in impatience, but Samantha was nowhere to be seen. When she finally turned the corner with a bedpan instead of the missing chart, Paul exploded. He screamed that she was an incompetent fool who should be fired. Instead, it was Paul who almost lost his job.

Paul had a tendency to judge others as either being like him and therefore worthy of respect or below him and undeserving. Too often, he based his appraisal on superficial attributes or just a feeling of being in sync. Samantha's relaxed nature contrasted with his type A fast-paced style and led Paul to completely discredit her.

Furthermore, Samantha's casual attitude had activated an old schema of Paul's in which people who should have been appreciative of his energy and quick thinking had, in fact, been completely unimpressed. Samantha's calm, steady ways reflected an air of self-confidence that challenged Paul's need to be in control. Without the protective shield of power-determined respect, Paul felt threatened that she might turn the tables on him and expose his lack of experience.

Rather than be the one who made the decisions, he would be the one answering to her. Somehow, her years of experience on the unit made him feel like an outsider who was not always welcome.

At the moment that Samantha came into his view with a bedpan instead of a chart, Paul's "all bad" drawer flew open. Rather than accept the flicker of self-doubt that he had erred and misplaced the chart, he jumped to the assumption that Samantha had been incapable of finding it. His unprocessed fury at being linked with mediocrity took over. Instead of wondering what had happened, he judged Samantha as being incompetent. Paul felt diminished through association and powerless to make the unit run the way he thought a top-notch unit should. At that moment, Samantha represented all the inadequacies and shortcomings that had made him rank the entire hospital as less prestigious than the one at which he had failed to receive an appointment. Having to put up with incompetent people like Samantha felt like an unfair punishment for his own shortcomings, and his disappointment in his own failings was directed entirely at her.

Denial prevented Paul from recognizing Samantha's established strengths and experience. Projection led Paul to see Samantha as the one who was incompetent. If Paul had not been overwhelmed by splitting, he might have been able to give Samantha the benefit of the doubt and learn the facts before reacting. He would have discovered that she had worked efficiently to try to locate the missing chart that was not, despite what he thought, on the rack by that or any other patient's door. Samantha had resigned herself to another one of Paul's rapidly reached conclusions that frequently led to errors and had taken advantage of the return to the nursing station to perform a duty that was outside of her job description but important for patient care and efficiency on the unit—a decision that was beyond the comprehension of this inexperienced, self-aggrandizing young physician.

Righting a Wrong

Perhaps you, like Paul, sometimes feel like something important to you has been taken away. Paul's black-and-white thinking led him to believe that hospitals were either wonderful or terrible and that being associated with a less prestigious organization meant that he was a loser. If Paul had been capable of noticing the tension in his body every time he walked through the doors or his intense physical reaction to Samantha, he might have been able to alert himself to an impending predicament. If he could have asked himself what he was feeling, he could have identified feeling deprived of what he felt he was entitled to, resentful about being perceived by others as being inferior, and enraged by not having control over the team he depended on. How different it might have been if Paul understood his tendency to split and flood and could challenge his thinking pattern when he noticed himself beginning to feel intolerant, indignant, or compromised. If Paul had learned to read his physical response to triggers, he would have recognized his rapid heartbeat and racing thoughts as warning signals that could have signaled to him that he should calm down before speaking. Without this self-knowledge, the brain chemistry aroused in Paul's amygdala caused him to assert himself in order to dominate but shut down the neural connections to the thinking parts of his brain that would have allowed him to challenge his perceptions and save his job.

Entitlement

Paul's predicament was also created by narcissistic tendencies and the entitlement that goes along with them. If work was only about accomplishments, then narcissism might actually be a good thing. To surpass goals, a narcissist will work long hours, take on challenges that seem daunting to others, and come up with creative solutions in order to beat the competition. However, there is a downside that can be as damaging to the work environment as it is to personal relationships.

Paul's need to establish his superiority may have pushed him to strive for high standards, which could be helpful at times, but it certainly didn't help him develop team skills. Even if you own your own company, narcissistic tendencies can still cause serious problems. If you tend to judge others too quickly, you may end up with simplistic categories for those coworkers you trust and those you for whom you have no respect. Your intolerance of incompetence may lead you to overreact to simple mistakes, damaging the confidence of employees who might have considerable talent and potential. When employees feel used rather than supported, their goodwill and commitment to your organization will dry up.

If you are not the boss, then things are even more problematic. Narcissistic defenses can make us view our own accomplishments in a one-sided way. Research has shown that narcissistic employees often feel entitled to promotions and rewards that they may not deserve (Judge, LePine, and Rich 2006; Penney and Spector 2002). Their efforts to succeed personally may come at the expense of others and may not even be in the best interests of the company. Whether you work by yourself or are part of a large organization, a narcissistic drive for perfection makes you extremely sensitive to failure and more likely to blame others when things don't go well.

Costly Implosions

Some of us have learned too well that it is better not to rock the boat. There are times when this is a strength, particularly when others are so emotionally charged that they are not capable of a thoughtful dialogue. But there are also times that we are simply not ready to challenge the situation, and so we try to avoid confronting the problem.

Burnout

Many of us use the word "burnout" to describe a state of dread about a job we wish we could quit. The thought of having to generate enough energy and enthusiasm to get through the week seems impossible, and we complain to others that we feel depleted, unappreciated, and unrewarded. Usually, there are specific incidents that have made us angry or upset, but instead of believing that the problem can be identified and corrected, we have shut those feelings down. Perhaps without even knowing why, we have given in to helplessness and hopelessness.

■ RUTH'S STORY

Ruth could see things at work going from bad to worse, but she decided to go to counseling the day she found herself watching the clock from the moment she first arrived, in a countdown to quitting time. She had to force herself back into the building after her lunch break and realized that she had taken more sick days in the previous month than she had in the six years she had worked there. In therapy, Ruth was asked to pinpoint the time when her attitude toward work started to change. She remembered that before her company merged, she had actually loved her job. She liked her projects and enjoyed working with her team. Her boss, Sandy, was demanding but fair and had helped her get a promotion just before the merger was announced. After the merger, her job description changed, and she was assigned to a different floor and reporting structure. Instead of having her own office with a window that provided plenty of sunshine for her plants, she had a small desk in a workstation that afforded little privacy and no exposure to the outside world.

Although she had initially been relieved that she would continue working with two of her former team members, she discovered that the men seemed to stick together but excluded her from their casual conversations. She had tried to insert herself in their shared jokes but gave up after a few weeks. When she had commented that their new supervisor was a real stickler for grammar, one of them had replied, "Guess Sandy won't be able to protect you anymore." Ruth realized that they had harbored resentment toward her close relationship with Sandy and obviously didn't think that she had deserved her promotion. From that day on, just seeing them or hearing their voices filled her with tension. She worried that they were out to get her and that instead of supporting her, they wanted her to fail. Ruth even started to wonder if her supervisor had covered up her weaknesses and if without Sandy's guidance and supervision she would be fired.

Ruth had cut herself off from so many important feelings. The merger had made everyone anxious about job security and the changes in personnel that were bound to occur. She had also felt grief that she would no longer be working with Sandy, for she had come to think of Sandy as a kind of aunt whom she could trust and rely on. Getting Sandy's approval had meant a great deal, and Ruth felt a void that was difficult to put into words. But when she saw her new office arrangement, she understood that there was no one there who could guide her or share her simple pleasure in things like noticing a new bloom on her plants. She felt that it wasn't fair that after six years she would have to start all over. When she realized that her coworkers were resentful and unsupportive, Ruth felt alone and vulnerable. She became more aware of the competitive nature of this new work environment and her inability to protect herself from an unanticipated source of aggression. Any one of these events would have been difficult enough to process, but together they pushed her into a state of emotional numbness.

How different it could have been if Ruth had been able to identify her feelings and ask herself if there were old emotional memories adding to the intensity. She would have realized that her new work situation had triggered childhood experiences that had never been fully worked through. The most important ones were connected to her experience of losing her best friend and social standing after her family moved across the country for her dad's new job. Ruth might have remembered that her parents were too busy to notice or help her deal with her loss and the challenges of being left out and eventually bullied by the kids in her new class. Ruth's passivity had led to a two-year nightmare that had reemerged to shadow the present in ways that left her powerless and emotionally overwhelmed.

Rejection at Work

While work is not a popularity contest, people need to feel a sense of belonging and acceptance. Even if you are the kind of person who likes to keep your personal and work lives separate, knowing how to build and foster relationships with the people you work with is important. At the end of the day, your coworkers are the ones who participate in group decisions that affect your own goals and opportunities. Even if your ideas are solid, if someone in the group with stronger relationship connections opposes your plan, chances are that the group will side against you. If being in control is one of your triggers, then things are set for you to overreact in ways that keep this vicious cycle in play.

Psychologists who specialize in the work environment have just started to explore the dynamic of rejection by work colleagues. While past research has explained how we react to harsh and punitive bosses, the new research explains that we are even more likely to react when we feel excluded or treated like a scapegoat by coworkers (Penhaligon, Louis, and Restubog 2009). When the work culture allows unbridled competition and jockeying for position, some employees will respond by becoming more assertive. Those who back away or implode may easily become targets for the unrest and anxiety that the entire group is struggling with. Being able to use our awareness and name our feelings allows us to think more clearly about the dynamics and to generate productive options that are not shadowed by unfortunate childhood experiences.

A Thoughtful Perspective

The more familiar we are with the kinds of dynamics that can lead us to an emotional overreaction at work, the better prepared we will be to manage it. Work involves relationships with others who may activate control struggles, criticize our performance, and compete in ways that breed envy and resentment. Work is also the arena where we test our own competence and efficacy and endure disappointment and, occasionally, failure. For many of us, the work we do is an important part of our identity and our financial security, as well as our self-esteem. Our emotional responses can be just as intense at work as in our private lives, and our need to stay calm while thoughtfully processing information is as vital to emotional health as it is to career.

Taking Responsibility

Overreactions can have a negative effect on the way you are perceived by others. If you've had a meltdown or explosion at work, you are better off taking responsibility for your behavior and attempting to repair relationships that have been affected than trying to ignore the situation. Most colleagues will appreciate a coworker who apologizes and admits to being under too much stress. Colleagues are more likely to let the incident pass if they realize that you truly regret making them the target for issues that didn't involve them. It is also important to take the first step in apologizing to your supervisor, boss, or clients who may have witnessed or heard about your overreaction. Taking this stance requires maturity and humility, which is exactly what you'll need to have in order to counteract any impressions that you are immature or have a sense of entitlement. You may not think that overreactions of the implosive kind create problems for others, but that is simply not the case. If you become withdrawn and moody, you bring that atmosphere with you. Cynicism and pessimism can bring down the spirits of coworkers and push people away. Taking responsibility by admitting that you haven't been managing your stress in the best way possible helps correct the image you project and opens up potential connections that could help you turn your situation around.

CHAPTER 11

Challenges at Home

Why is it that we have one set of rules regarding the way we treat the people we work or socialize with and another for the people who mean the most to us? Sometimes we can admit that it's easier to let off steam when we don't have to face the reprimands or consequences in a job setting, but most people I know deeply regret the times their overreactions have hurt their partners, parents, or children.

Daily Life

Being part of a family automatically reminds us of the memories formed during our childhood. Triggers related to criticism, envy, rejection, and control are easily activated even though the people involved are completely different. Shared living almost always guarantees that we will have to face the same demands and issues that created turmoil when we were young. We may be older and wiser, but we are not always prepared for the emotional minefield we navigate on a daily basis. Each time we step on an emotionally charged mine, we are swept back into expectations, emotional memories, and childhood beliefs that haven't been thoroughly resolved. Once the brain has processed an event as a danger, the stage for overreaction has been set.

Costly Implosions

If your childhood experiences make it difficult for you to express your point of view and risk conflict, then you may find yourself avoiding problems until you are over your limit.

■ SARAH'S STORY

Last week Sarah called to cancel an appointment she had for marital therapy with her husband, Rob. "I just don't think this will ever work, and I don't have the energy to keep on trying. I've been thinking about divorce for almost two years now, and I don't want to put it off any longer." I coaxed Sarah to keep our appointment and asked what had led to her despair. Sarah started to speak about their daughter's soccer game and how badly Rob had behaved. The kids had been overscheduled that day and needed two parents to rush one child to a baseball game while the other child was taken home to shower and then on to a music lesson. As soon as the last whistle had blown, Rob was anxious to get to Sarah's car in order to retrieve the baseball equipment and water bottles he had prom-ised to bring for the team. She found herself scurrying behind him, arms overfilled with practice balls, half-finished snacks, and their son's backpack. The worst part was when Rob found the car door locked and snarled at her to hurry up so that he wouldn't be late for the game. At that moment, the story of her marriage coalesced. She would be overburdened, taken for granted, and forced to answer to him. Her own dream of having a partner who would gallantly offer to share in carrying the kids' belongings and make her feel appreciated would shrink until it was invisible.

In therapy, I was able to explore how that one harried moment of switching equipment at a car had unleashed hundreds of memories of times when Rob and other family members had placed burdens on her without seeming to notice or care about her. How different it might have been if Sarah had paid attention to the way she felt as she started to pull belongings together at the end of the game. She might have noticed her stomach twisting into knots at the sight of Rob casually turning his back. If she had been able to name her feelings, she might have known that she resented the way he assumed that she would do all the work. She might have noticed first a fleeting wish that someone would see that she needed help and then the way she checked her urge to call Rob and the children back to her side and demand that they help. If she had noticed these feelings and thoughts, she might have been able to ask herself to name the old emotional memories that were stopping her.

In therapy, Sarah was able to identify the feelings and themes that culminated in her decision to pursue a divorce. Even though Sarah knew she felt overextended and taken for granted, she was not comfortable asking for help or complaining when others didn't volunteer to help her out. Instead, Sarah displayed a veneer of capability and preferred to view herself as being self-sufficient and capable. When I asked Sarah if she had always been like that, she assured me that she had been that way all her life. Sarah could rattle off stories of winning tournament trophies and buying her own clothes but had difficulty coming up with memories of being taken care of by her parents. If anything, the roles had been switched. Sarah told me that she had learned to cook and do the laundry when she was nine years old, and she remembered making lunches for both herself and her mother. She didn't want to blame her mother and tried not to think about how difficult their lives became after her father's unilateral decision to get a divorce a few weeks after Sarah's eighth birthday. Sarah's mother had managed to find a job that helped them survive financially but was so exhausted and depressed by her situation that she let the burden of household responsibilities fall on Sarah. Even worse, Sarah's mother would go to bed right after dinner and cry herself to sleep every night.

Sarah had lost a great deal of respect for both of her parents, believing that her mother's emotional neediness had been part of the reason her father had left. Sarah still loved her father but had privately concluded that men who were faced with too many demands would walk out the door. Until I helped Sarah connect the dots, she had never considered how her own childhood burdens made her want to protect her own children from having any responsibilities. By not repeating her mother's neediness and ensuring that neither her husband nor her children would have any demands, Sarah was perpetuating a cycle where she could never be taken care of. Without knowing that it was safe to ask for help, she was repeating a past that filled her with resentment and despair.

Once it was openly explored, Rob was able to apologize for being so focused on getting to the baseball game that he hadn't noticed her struggle. But he also insisted that he would have been glad to help her carry the soccer balls if she had asked for help. It just didn't occur to him that she was having a hard time. By the end of that session the couple was talking about ways to check in with each other that might prevent this kind of stress, and when they walked out, Sarah was smiling at the man she had wanted to divorce just an hour before.

Self-Sufficiency

Too many people find themselves in Sarah's predicament, where their obligations and responsibilities have taken over their lives. Like Sarah, they have grown up not really trusting that others will be there to share their load. Being part of a new family offers the opportunity to try doing things differently. Even if you didn't have parents who were there to notice and step in when you needed help, that doesn't mean that this pattern will be impossible to break. If you are exhausted by responsibilities, it's hard not to overreact.

Costly Explosions

Life is full of disappointments and times when things simply go wrong. People forget to set their alarm clocks, dogs get into garbage, and milk expires. But instead of learning to help each other and working together to solve these problems or find a humorous perspective, some families erupt with tension that is partly created by the need to find fault.

■ ETHAN AND OLIVIA'S STORY

Ethan and Olivia knew that they each tended toward perfectionism but were relatively happy in the first few years of their marriage.

Both found good jobs after they graduated law school, and they celebrated their first anniversary believing that they would be happy forever. Things changed dramatically when Olivia quit her job after their son was born and Ethan learned that his chances of advancing in his law firm were weak. With school loans and a mortgage on their new condominium, both were feeling the pinch of financial stress.

Olivia knew that Ethan needed to put in extra hours at his job, but she secretly believed that his tendency to be forgetful was largely to blame for his lack of success, as well as the extra time he spent at work in order to wrap up projects. A typical argument erupted when Ethan was rushing out the door in the morning only to discover that the car battery was dead. He scurried back and announced to Olivia that he would miss his train to work if she didn't drop what she was doing and drive him to the station. Olivia needed to get their son ready for preschool and both were still in their pajamas. Annoyed by Ethan's tone of voice, Olivia coldly responded that things would be a little easier on the whole family if he could remember to make sure the car doors were properly closed before he went to bed at night. With that, Ethan exploded in a rage, saying that Olivia always assumed that everything was his fault and that he'd be happy to be in his pajamas right now if she was willing to get a job. Within minutes, both were screaming at the top of their lungs, the baby was crying, and the commuter train had come and gone.

Better Resolutions

When we have difficulty tolerating feelings such as guilt, inadequacy, or shame, we may feel angry at the other person who is involved in the situation. Instead of recognizing that our own disappointment or sense of failure has awakened painful emotional memories, we think that the person who expressed a need or injury has done something purposeful to make us feel bad. While it's easy to "shoot the messenger," it creates unnecessary tension. The person whose needs are expressed ends up being attacked, and a problem that might have been easily resolved gets lost in the eruption that follows.

So many couples come to therapy because they feel that their needs and hopes cannot be safely expressed. The belief that you have no voice is a dangerous one, as it awakens triggers of being neglected, having no control, and feeling unimportant. Adults who turn shame or guilt into rage have difficulty hearing their children or even tolerating situations that might lead them to a happier outcome. The pursuit of blame prevents us from registering the lesson that needs to be learned and offering our support to help others restore goodwill. Situations that aren't resolved tend to breed resentment and flare up as quickly as a forest fire in a drought.

Taking Responsibility

Perhaps you can identify with the reactions to feeling neglected, misunderstood, or blamed described in the stories in this chapter. Many of the parents and couples I work with have also found that these are the triggers that have led them to withdraw (implode) or start a battle (explode). In chapters 12 and 13, I will help you consider ways to prevent overreactions, but it is also important to think about how to take responsibility when you have already overreacted and have hurt someone you care about.

Resolving an overreaction can be just as meaningful to you as it is to the person you would like to mend things with. It can only happen when you are able to respond in a thoughtful way that indicates you have been able to reflect on the trigger, identify your feelings, and sort through the defenses and emotional memories that have most likely pushed you into such an extreme state. Your ability to show this more thoughtful self to the people who experienced your overreaction can be beneficial to everyone involved. Mending hurt feelings and disappointments allows you to bring important ingredients to the relationships you value the most. When the capacity to empathize or apologize is scarce in a family, everyone suffers, but as people begin to benefit from the strong emotional resource of feeling cared about and understood, everyone will become better able to provide this when others are in need. You may be the one offering this gift today but enjoying it when it is given to you tomorrow.

Mending an overreaction with the people we love is also an important way to defuse the feelings before they are filed away in the memory drawer of other events that ended badly. If the events filed in the "all bad" drawer had been properly mended to begin with, they wouldn't have ended up in that drawer. And offering an apology and acknowledging that your reaction was over the top will help your family members or friends defuse *their* emotions so that they are less likely to add this altercation to other resentments they may harbor.

To allow this experience to work for both of you, remember that your overreaction has most likely been created by (or been part of) another person's overreaction. Just as we all have different boiling points, we all have different patterns of simmering down. If you try to mend things when you are calm but the other person is still very angry, your attempts will be rebuffed.

Try the following to help your efforts succeed:

- Make sure you are truly calm when you decide to start.

- Remember that your purpose is to mend a relationship rupture, not to show that you were right.

- Ask if your friend or family member is calm enough to speak with you about resolving the incident. If this person still seems emotionally reactive, explain that you would really like to try to mend this and that maybe the two of you could try to talk again when both of you have had enough time to create a little distance from the emotions.

- Protect your amygdala. You will get emotionally stimulated all over again if you sense danger. Try to remember to scan for those physical responses you learned about in chapter 2 that indicate you are moving into a state of high arousal. If you notice that you are having those responses, you can end an unproductive conversation before it escalates into another overreaction.

- Keep your goal in sight. Establishing a conversation in which you are calm and receptive can make all the difference in the world. Remember the exercise you did in chapter

2 to learn how to make connections? It is easier to provide interest and empathy when a person is describing an event that doesn't involve you at all; when people start to tell you what you have done to hurt them, it is more challenging to listen without feeling blamed. To mend an overreaction, you need to shift your focus away from yourself and onto the person you wish to mend things with. If you can listen without interrupting and can identify one or two feelings that the person may have been experiencing, you have taken a huge step in the right direction.

If we are not able to repair the damage we create when we overreact, we are more likely to experience guilt, shame, or self-blame, which, in turn, can add to the patterns that contributed to the overreaction in the first place.

SECTION 4

New Strategies

By now you have learned a lot about what is happening in your mind and body when you overreact. You have evaluated your own response patterns and thought about areas you are particularly sensitive about. Through the exercises and stories of others, you have seen how tension, stress, and old emotional beliefs can work against your better judgment. Finally, you have considered examples of triggers that many people encounter at work and in their personal lives. In this section you will learn how to put all of this information together to find new ways of preventing and dealing with episodes of overreaction.

CHAPTER 12

Getting Centered

Overreactions are a product of brain chemistry, emotional memories, schema-based expectations, and unhelpful defense mechanisms. The most important thing you can do when you sense that you might be overreacting is to momentarily distance yourself from the situation that has triggered your reaction and try to calm down. Sometimes that might involve physically removing yourself from a situation, particularly if there is a risk that your reaction could be dangerous to anyone. At other times, your only option will be to create a psychological boundary so that you can find a different mind-set through which to think and feel. In this chapter, I will review the importance of getting *centered*, which means returning to a state of emotional equilibrium. It also involves learning to thoughtfully explore your reaction until you have a clear understanding of your feelings and the situation that triggered that reaction. You can reach a state of emotional equilibrium only when you have identified the emotional memories that are adding to the intensity of the experience and found ways to challenge any defensive splitting or flooding that may have been activated.

Identify the Changes in Your Body

When your amygdala is activated, altered brain chemistry produces physiological responses that you can learn to identify. Adrenaline and cortisol put us into a state of agitation that has been described as *diffuse physiological arousal.* Our activated central nervous system creates changes in our heart rate, breathing, and gut (Schore 2002). As we ready ourselves to fight or flee, our energy surges into our muscles, preparing us for a physical response while at the same time making it almost impossible to process information. This state of response is actually experienced throughout your body, and it is your signal that your amygdala has started to fire. While your attention may be directed to the problem that has triggered your response, it is far more important to pay attention to these symptoms.

The body scan exercise in chapter 2 helped you become familiar with your physical response style. You learned to notice how different parts of your body felt when you were relaxed and to identify the way your body changed when you thought about specific emotional memories. Your ability to scan and register changes in your body can be extremely helpful to you in preventing overreactions. Every time your brain perceives a threat to your well-being, the information registers throughout your body. The earlier you can catch yourself being thrown off balance, the easier it is to find your center again.

The next time you are in a stressful situation, check to see if you experience any of the following:

- feeling stiff or tight in your neck

- feeling flushed or hot

- having a quickening or rapid heartbeat

- feeling queasy or like you've been punched in the stomach

- starting to sweat

- having clammy palms

- feeling numb

- being unable to concentrate

- feeling distracted or preoccupied by uninvited or racing thoughts

Knowing your body's response style to arousal is one of the most important tools you can develop. Once you know your own response style, you can be more alert to the subtle but very meaningful changes that tell you it's time to use everything you have learned about overreacting.

Calm Down

Once your body has alerted you that you are in a state of high arousal, your priority is to return to a state of emotional equilibrium. There are different exercises and strategies that you can try, and it's impossible to predict which one will work best for you (Augustine and Hemenover 2009). Some of these suggestions might sound weird or unlike anything you have ever considered doing before. Perhaps you have heard of some of them but just don't see the point. Try to stay open to strategies that have worked for others. After all, what do you really have to lose?

Picture Your Brain Functions

Remember that different parts of your brain manage emotions, memories, and judgment. When the connections between these parts shut down, you can't access all of the ingredients that you need in order to handle the situation in the best way. When you are in a moment of high arousal, just stopping to think about what is happening in your brain can help generate the awareness and self-reflection that can help turn things around.

Left and Right

Imagine that you are in a lab where you can have a brain scan. Picture an image that shows how the right side of your brain is all lit up. Notice that the left side isn't showing any activity at all. Message your amygdala to let it know that it's done its job for the moment. Let the left brain know that you need a little help right now trying to figure out what's really going on. You might say something like, "Okay amygdala, I know that something's up, but can you just slow down for one minute so I can try to figure it out? Left brain…where are you? I need help naming this feeling so things don't get out of hand."

Bottom and Top

Imagine that your brain scan shows that the lower part of your brain is all lit up. Notice that the higher brain functions are completely blacked out. Remind yourself that this is a dangerous picture and that following your impulses usually leads to actions you later regret. Talk to the thinking part of your brain so that your experience can add a grain of wisdom. You might say something like, "Okay instincts, I hear you. But let's see if my experience agrees that this is the best decision. Is this something that I will regret later?"

Snap Out of It

Wear an elastic band around your wrist. When you feel that you are entering a state of high arousal, snap the band so that it stings. A physical distraction like this allows some people to divert their attention from negative thoughts back to their body. By taking action, you transfer from a passive position into one of action and agency. Your effort to take control of the situation can keep you focused on regaining your equilibrium and help you remember the next steps you need to take in order to avoid a knee-jerk reaction.

Name Your Feelings

Pushing yourself to identify and name your feelings is an important part of getting grounded. In chapter 2, you were asked to become familiar with dozens of different feeling states that contribute to overall experiences of anger, contentment, or insecurity. Drs. Matthew Lieberman and Naomi Eisenberger (Lieberman et al. 2007) have demonstrated how helpful that exercise can be in a moment of emotional intensity. When research subjects were asked to label the feeling that best fit a series of powerful images, their efforts to concentrate on selecting the best description immediately diminished the activity in the amygdala and related regions. As the thinking parts of the brain connect to your emotional response, you will be better able to move beyond that first impulse to either implode or explode.

Breathe

Another strategy for getting centered comes from the mindfulness approach to emotional distress (Williams and Teasdale 2007). Mindfulness is an offshoot of Buddhist meditation and combines mindful philosophy with breathing techniques. *Mindful practice* takes us away from the tendency to overthink and asks us to suspend judgment as we invest all of our energy in the experience of being fully aware of how it feels to be in this particular moment in time. As Drs. Ruth Baer and Debra Huss (2008) point out, the mindful approach requires acceptance of the wide range of sensations and feelings that people experience. From this perspective, emotions are just states that will come and go if we don't allow ourselves to get too agitated by them. If we can accept them as sensations and information, their urgency passes and they are replaced by other states.

In a proper mindfulness exercise, your mind is free to roam from thought to thought while you simply observe yourself in the experience. To move beyond a state of turbulence, something as simple as focusing on your breath can help you return to the moment. When you concentrate on how your body feels as you inhale and exhale, thoughts and feelings may flicker into awareness. Acknowledging those thoughts and feelings is not at all similar to obsessing or ruminating over the problem that has triggered your reaction. Tuning your thoughts back to your breath will allow your emotions to ebb and flow.

As you inhale deeply, follow the movement of the fresh air as it travels through your nasal passages, throat, and chest and into your abdomen. As you breathe out, exhale some of the tension that has been building inside of you. Just concentrate on your breath and breathe deeply and slowly. Focus on how different parts of your body feel as you move through a breathing cycle. If thoughts or feelings creep into your awareness, remind yourself that emotional states come and go and that it will be easier to know what to do when you're not blinded by emotion.

Many people find this approach helpful during moments of agitation and even more useful after they have learned to build mindful exercises into their daily lives. Like other techniques, learning to shift your focus away from obsessive thinking is more effective and easier to do if you have practiced it in moments of calm.

Use Guided Imagery

While some incidents of overreaction are over in a flash, many people find themselves worked up for hours or even days. They tend to ruminate on the trigger and, as a result, constantly reemerge into states of heightened arousal and intensity. While you might not have the time or privacy to count on guided imagery as your first resort in a moment of crisis, it is a wonderful option to employ as soon as you have a private moment.

In chapter 2, you were asked to experiment with the power of positive emotional memories through an exercise in guided imagery. You learned how to recall a specific event and shift your concentration to the things you remembered seeing, feeling, smelling, and hearing. Just remembering the details of this wonderful experience has the power to revive your emotional memory and the sense of well-being that you had in that moment. Knowing which memory works best to soothe you or restore your self-confidence makes it easier to turn to that memory when you are ready to open the "good" drawer of your emotional filing cabinet and immerse yourself in the positive. When you choose to do this, you are truly using your mind to switch your response pattern.

Challenge Your Perception

Once you find a way to interrupt the escalating response, you need to check for the possibility that your interpretations and conclusions may be suspect. You may be sufficiently aware of your triggers to know that one has been activated, but it may take some time before you can think clearly enough to know that for sure. There are things you can do to help this process.

Acknowledge Your General Situation

Research has shown that when we are sleep deprived or under a lot of stress, we are more prone to emotional overreactions. Brain-imaging studies collected by Drs. Matthew Walker and Els van der Helm (2009) show that healthy, competent people who have been sleep deprived have a 60 percent increase in levels of amygdala activity when they are exposed to situations that evoke negative reactions. Even more important, the connections between the amygdala and the thinking parts of the brain appear to fade, while the connections between the automatic or knee-jerk response system and the amygdala get stronger. Similar studies have found changes in brain chemistry and neural imbalances when people are under persistent stress.

If you know that you are exhausted or have been under a lot of pressure, chances are that you are overaroused and poorly equipped to manage a negative encounter. Rather than persist, ask yourself if there's any way to simply defer until you are better equipped to deal with the problem. One woman I worked with found herself easily agitated in the hours before her bedtime. She learned to recognize that arguments started in that time period were guaranteed to get out of control, so she decided to tell herself that she would do a better job resolving the issue in the morning. She was able to bring a fresh perspective and a more emotionally balanced self to the conversation after a good night's rest and was delighted with her ability to handle things in a way that brought her respect from others, on top of good results.

Search for Splitting and Flooding

Although the exact sequence of events is not completely understood, a state of heightened arousal is frequently accompanied or triggered by anxiety. Anxiety also has the power to activate our defense mechanisms so that our perception becomes clouded. When we start to see things as all or nothing, we are in a full-blown episode of splitting. The thoughts and feelings that are generated from this position have much more to do with the past and former incidents that have been stored in our emotional filing cabinet than with anything happening in the present.

Frequently, splitting causes us to have a very strong reaction. While some of the people I work with describe it as intensity, others say that it seems like someone has flicked a switch. The thoughts that are produced when we are splitting tend to be completely one-sided and extreme. Often this takes the form of overgeneralizations, such as "always" or "never" and other kinds of black-and-white thinking. Splitting usually leads to flooding, which is sometimes easier to identify. When you suddenly find yourself remembering other instances that confirm your evaluation, you have started to flood.

The second exercise in chapter 5 helped you figure out if you are the kind of person who tends to think in all-or-nothing terms under certain circumstances. Many overreactions are the product of splitting and flooding that combine to distort our thinking. After you have used one of the techniques described above to help you focus on the present, there are some important questions to ask yourself: "Am I looking at things through the lens of splitting? Am I thinking about things in terms of best and worst, all or nothing? Am I thinking back to other times when something like this happened? Am I saying things like, 'He *always*' or 'I *never*'?" Remember, the conclusions you reach under the influence of splitting and flooding cannot be trusted. They are always one-sided and extreme. If you catch yourself in the moment, you can spend your energy calming down rather than working yourself up based on "facts" that often end up being one-sided and inaccurate and won't lead you to a constructive solution.

■ ANDY'S STORY

Andy's business has really gone downhill over the past year, and he has had to give up the lease on his office space. His primary account dried up, and he's been toying with ideas that involve shifting the focus of his product and approaching companies he worked with years ago. He's also considering starting a new business with a partner who has expertise in advertising, which would complement his own background. Andy told me that he's had a hard time focusing this week. When he starts to think about all the possibilities and all the things he has to do, he just feels overwhelmed. In the old days he would try to distract himself by tuning out the stress and turning on the solitaire. These days he's trying to stick with his emotions and fight his tendency to split.

Andy knows that he has started to see things from a negative perspective when he makes self-defeating critiques of all his plans. It starts with a feeling of being lost or confused. Instead of feeling that he is engaged in the moment and moving forward with an idea or a plan, it feels like he is stuck and spinning around. In the background, he is aware of negative beliefs like "You never had the discipline to write out a business plan the right way before. What makes you think you can do it now?" He thinks about what needs to get done and believes that he doesn't have the skills he should have acquired by now. This style of beating himself up for his inadequacies starts with an inability to focus and a sense that he is drifting from idea to idea instead of making progress. He has too many thoughts and a vague sense of being overwhelmed. Some of those thoughts are about things he would rather be doing and distractions that might feel like a better use of time. Only after staying with a thought long enough to register it can Andy recognize that he is sending himself highly critical messages. When Andy does a body scan, he realizes that his stomach is in knots and his heart is beating more quickly than it normally does. After he works on calming down, Andy can see how the anxiety made him feel disorganized, confused, and overwhelmed. When he feels calm, he can allow himself to focus on one project and set a realistic goal for what could be accomplished in that period of time. Andy left knowing that he had to put more emphasis on the body scan and on trying exercises to reduce tension as soon as he notices it. It also helped Andy to know that when he is calm again, he is able to focus and the negative thinking disappears.

Subdue Emotional Memories

Although I strongly believe that we can learn from the past, the experience of being flooded by emotional memories is neither educational nor helpful. In many ways it is more similar to opening Pandora's box. Pandora is a character in Greek mythology who was given many gifts by the gods, including a box that she was instructed not to open. She became curious one day and decided to open the lid. Suddenly, all of the evils, diseases, and burdens that had never existed in the world before were released.

In chapter 5, I explained how certain schemas are stored in the "all good" or "all bad" drawer of our mental filing cabinets. Once a folder has been opened, there is the potential for all the other emotional memories related to the underlying schema to become reactivated. To make matters worse, folders that have similar themes can also be stirred up, so that hundreds of unprocessed painful emotional experiences can jump into a situation that is already stressful enough.

I have advised my clients that it is wiser to close Pandora's box. I tell them that they have a choice: to let these emotional memories overtake the moment or to decide to put them back in the box. In the next chapter, we will look at helpful ways to work with emotional memories, but in the middle of an episode where you are splitting and flooding, it is best to put them back in the box and close the lid.

One way to accomplish this is to create a mantra that helps you stop registering past incidents. A simple phrase that helps you focus on what's happening in the moment can be a powerful reminder. One man I recently worked with discovered that the phrase "Stick with the story" reminded him to close the Pandora's box that held his accumulated resentments. A woman who was fighting to undo the influence of a difficult childhood chose to say to herself, "This isn't who I want to be." This was all she needed to say to be reminded of the self she wished to become. Perhaps one of these mantras will connect with you. If not, take a moment when you are calm to write down one sentence that will be powerful enough to stop you in your tracks when old emotional memories start to invade the moment. If you can do this, it's amazing how much clearer you will be, enabling you to move on to the next steps.

Create Options

When we are overwhelmed by emotional memories and unhelpful defenses, our belief system is heavily influenced by schemas of other situations that didn't turn out well. Without realizing it, we may be narrowing the field to exclude alternatives and options that would allow things to move in an entirely different direction. There are things that we can do to reverse this process.

Don't Brood

A thoughtful approach is one that integrates beliefs, thoughts, and feelings but does not allow the focus to shift to rumination. When your thoughts keep returning to a problem, your amygdala will keep firing (Bushman 2002). Because this part of your brain is primed to help you act in order to get yourself out of danger, brooding just keeps the sense of danger constantly with you. This creates a vicious cycle that keeps you hypervigilant and emotionally stressed.

Many people who ruminate have traits that psychologists label as neuroticism. *Neuroticism* leads people to construe events in negative ways, be more hesitant to make important decisions, feel uncomfortable with uncertainty, and take longer periods of time to respond to troubling situations (Phelps and LeDoux 2005; Suls and Martin 2005). Whether this trait is acquired through genetics, family dynamics, life events, or some combination isn't fully understood, but researchers do know that allowing this pattern to dominate your personality leads to heightened episodes of anxiety and helplessness (Hirsh and Inzlicht 2008). If you see yourself as carrying these traits, it is time to confront yourself and challenge responses that were acquired in childhood. Your brain is capable of opening new pathways if you will only give yourself the chance. When Drs. Rebecca Ray and Kevin Ochsner (Ray et al. 2005) instructed ruminators to stop brooding about a threatening situation in order to pay attention to the next task, they switched gears easily, giving their emotional network a chance to calm down. Within minutes, they were completely focused on the task at hand and responding just like the research subjects who did not have neurotic tendencies.

Keep Goals in Sight

Research has shown that we are better able to control our impulses when the part of our brain that holds long-term goals is kept active (Cyders and Smith 2008; Grawe 2007; Moses and Barlow 2006). When disturbing emotions erupt, we need all the help we can find to make sure that our responses will be thoughtful or purposeful. Our ability to remind ourselves of what is truly important is a strong antidote for impulses that are entirely based on unprocessed emotions. The power of the future will be discussed more fully in chapter 13, but your ability to hold on to the awareness of the positive parts of your life is very important.

Telling yourself how you ought to feel or reciting what you think you should believe is not the same thing, and it doesn't seem to work. When people who don't feel good about themselves are told to give themselves a pep talk and say things like "I can succeed" or "I am worthy of love," it often backfires and makes them feel worse. However, being able to hold the memory or belief of a time when you felt very capable or very secure reminds you that things can turn out that way again. In the same way, reminding yourself of something that you believe you can achieve in the immediate future helps you steer your expectations away from negative thinking. I have found this to be helpful for the clients I work with. Being able to shift focus from old emotional pains to present or future opportunities helps shake the sense of being overwhelmed that is generated when we lose our sense of efficacy and succumb to helplessness.

Use Props

One technique that can help you shift focus in this way is to create a symbol that represents your most important goal. While mantras can be used for this purpose, it is also possible to carry or wear an item that helps you focus on what you really want. I worked with a successful businessman whose marriage was in shambles. He discovered that looking at his wedding band helped him remember that his wife would simply not tolerate any more abuse and that keeping his family intact was the most important thing in the world to him. A woman who was working on controlling her temper around her child found that wearing a bracelet her child had made for her in kindergarten reminded her of how badly she wanted to keep their relationship based on love and caring. The symbolic object you choose is not intended to become a good luck charm or to hold magical powers, but feeling it or seeing it can remind you of your most important goals.

Use Reinforcements

Many people who are working on major changes find that daily meetings help them keep their goals in perspective. This is true for many people who benefit from Alcoholics Anonymous (AA) or Narcotics Anonymous (NA) and also for people who draw their strength from a religious or spiritual affiliation. Frequent shared affirmation of goals that you believe in helps keep those goals in sight what you encounter a setback or challenge. Just acknowledging your goals is enough to reconnect the pathways in your brain that loosen the amygdala's grip.

Change the Ending

Neural imaging studies have highlighted the importance of how we think about the situations we face. Negative emotions such as fear and anger that start in the amygdala can be quieted when the situation is appraised from a different perspective. If you dwell on the problem and ruminate about all its negative aspects, the activity in your amygdala will continue at full force. But there are mental exercises that help shift the focus and allow an entirely different part of your brain to take over. To test this out, Drs. Rebecca Ray and Kevin Ochsner, and their associates at Stanford University (Ray et al. 2005) showed people pictures of stressful events such as an impending car accident. When the research subjects were told to imagine that scenario happening to them or to someone they loved, they became very upset. However, when researchers instructed them to think of a positive outcome or a way to make it better, the left prefrontal area of the brain was activated and the amygdala calmed down. Challenging negative expectations changes the way we feel and creates the emotional energy we need to turn things around. It seems that when we take a proactive stance and focus on what is doable instead of on impending harm, our brain works in ways that help us calm down.

Reach Out

Many therapists believe that the circuits between the thinking and feeling parts of our brain can be strengthened through close relationships (Fishbane 2007; Schore and Schore 2008; Siegel and Hartzell 2003). Unhelpful defense mechanisms surge when we feel abandoned and diminish when we feel secure. Connecting with the people who care about you can help you get through emotional storms and can provide long-lasting benefits as well. Research and clinical practice suggest that what you really need is an opportunity to restore your sense of security so that you can regain your emotional equilibrium. As children we benefit from being soothed and reassured, and we never really outgrow the relief that comes from knowing that we're not alone.

When you turn to others for help, there are a number of ways you can approach them to get what you need. Too often, we sabotage ourselves when trying to get what we truly need. When we reach out to others and ask them to help us solve a problem, we are using our left brain to engage another person's left brain. That person might respond by presenting ideas and solutions without even noticing the emotional distress underlying the question. At the end of that kind of exchange, our need for security may have been only partially met or not met at all, leading to additional emotional distress. If we try to take control and use our power to make sure other people give us what we need, we often cause our loved ones to pull away. Our intensity and power tactics rarely create empathic or caring responses. When we don't realize that the way we have requested comfort has sabotaged the response, it's easy to conclude that people are withholding or uncaring. Even worse, we may have stimulated additional emotional memories of times when other people we turned to for comfort were not willing to supply it to us. Too often, the extra disappointment leads to more emotional distress, and we may end up unleashing our frustration on people we love.

Instead, we need to focus on an approach that allows us to communicate what we need in a way that is open and respectful. When you reach out, start by telling the person that something upsetting has happened to you and that it would be really helpful if he could give you a few minutes of support. Ask this person if this is a good time to talk or if he is in the middle of something else. A person who is preoccupied with an interrupted task won't be able to focus on you, and that may come across as being dismissive. It's better to make a plan to talk at a time that will allow you to get what you really need.

If someone is able to speak with you, explain that you're not looking for advice on how to handle the problem but that you're feeling overwhelmed or upset. You can also help steer the conversation in the right way by saying that you would feel better knowing that someone is there for you or that right now you just need a physical or emotional hug. Often, knowing that someone is there to listen and assure you that you are cared about is enough to take the sting away. If there is no one in your life right now who can be there for you, consider joining a group or reaching out to a therapist. The connections you build may make all the difference in learning to manage overwhelming emotions.

Knee-Jerk vs. Thoughtful Responses

Overreactions begin with a knee-jerk response to a specific trigger that we may not even recognize at the time. If something about the situation causes us to experience a sense of danger or injury, then our brain circuitry bypasses reflection and springs right into action. Often the trigger has unleashed tacit beliefs and expectations that lead us to evaluate things as being far more extreme than they truly are. If anxiety activates splitting and flooding, then the situation becomes more intolerable and we are inundated with painful emotional memories that add to the intensity of the moment.

In contrast, thoughtful reactions can only occur when we are able to acknowledge and reflect on all of the important ingredients: the trigger, the beliefs that have shaped our interpretation, and the emotional state that has been aroused. To do this, start with an understanding of how different emotional states feel. Attune yourself to the changes in your body that occur when the amygdala responds to perceived danger. Understanding that your body is in a state of high arousal, you can turn to one of the exercises you know will help you regain emotional equilibrium. You can picture your brain, name your feeling state, or use breathing techniques, guided imagery, or mantras to lessen the grip of intense emotions. You can also evaluate your general condition and remind yourself to proceed with caution if you are tired, run-down, or under too much stress.

As you return to the moment, focus on your inner experience in order to differentiate whether you are experiencing envy, humiliation, rejection, betrayal, helplessness, or something else. Rather than run from an emotional state, stay focused in order to clarify your internal experience. The process of thoughtful reflection will open up your brain circuits so that your energy won't be caught up maintaining a state of high arousal.

Assess your thoughts to see if you are splitting (seeing things as being one-sided) or flooding (having a surge of memories of similar situations). Ask if you have taken the time to get a full perspective or if you might be jumping to conclusions. If there is evidence of this, pause to recognize just how one-sided your thoughts and feelings are.

Ask yourself if you fully understand the event that has triggered your response. More often than not, it will be another example of a theme you have identified in previous chapters of this book. It is extremely important to identify this theme, for it is almost always connected to an emotional memory that is adding to the intensity of the situation.

In a thoughtful approach, you'll recognize the power of your beliefs and know how important it is to free yourself from old scenarios that may have nothing to do with the present. Remember Pandora's box and choose to put those memories away so that they can't add to your pain in the moment. Also challenge any negative expectations based on these memories and instead remind yourself that it can often be more important to focus on the present and future.

When you feel bombarded by feelings you don't comprehend, make time to talk out or write out your thoughts so that you can identify your internal experience. However, you need to make sure that your efforts to understand your feelings don't lead to obsessing about the details or ruminating about the situation. Brooding will only make it worse, and your time is better spent challenging a perspective that may be perpetuating the negative spin. Turn to people who care about you for support and encouragement and choose to use your free time doing something that will help you feel restored and cared about.

Knee-jerk reactions originate in the amygdala and are fueled by schemas, expectations, and memories that complicate and intensify your response. If your anxiety activates splitting and flooding, then your reaction becomes even more intense. When you put your energy into restoring your emotional equilibrium, you are empowering yourself to become calmer and more grounded. Only when you are certain that you have moved out of emotional arousal and have regained a balanced perspective can you trust that your reaction is safe—for you and for those you care about.

End-of-Chapter Exercise: Neurotic Tendencies

While no one wants to be labeled neurotic, our genetic predispositions, early childhood experiences, and acquired beliefs can create vulnerabilities that make us more emotionally sensitive than we need to be. One way to remedy this involves exploring and challenging our relationships with anxiety.

Part 1

Are these experiences almost always, often, or rarely true for you?

- I worry that I won't do things correctly.

- It is hard for me to relax without taking drugs or alcohol.

- I second-guess myself after I've decided to buy something or have committed to a plan.

- I have more doubts and worries than other people seem to have.

- People describe me as being moody.

- I am thin-skinned or very sensitive.

- Uncertainty makes me nervous.

- I prefer not to take risks.

- I think about my problems without intending to.

If these experiences are always or often true for you, then you have a response pattern that may be contributing to overreactions.

Part 2

While some of us may be born with heightened sensitivity, many of these patterns are passed down from our parents or exacerbated by early childhood experiences with them.

Were the following experiences almost always, often, or rarely true for either or both of your parents?

- They complained about my smallest failings.

- They filled the house with worry and tension.

- They were critical of each other or other relatives.

- They were overprotective of me.

- They didn't really know how to help me feel better when I was down or upset.

- They would get extremely upset or angry in ways that frightened or upset me.

- They tended to be pessimistic or negative thinkers.

- They got upset when routines were disrupted.

- They worried a lot about me and other family members.

- They didn't have as much fun as other parents seemed to have.

If you answered that one or both of your parents frequently responded this way, then you may have learned a response style that works against you. Remember, our beliefs and expectations are created when we are very young, but as adults, we have a choice. Our parents probably would have chosen to do things differently if that choice was given to them. Fear of the unknown and self-doubt work to erode our sense of efficacy and the energy we need to move forward in life. You will have to work to undo the power of your schemas and emotional memories, but if you are motivated to free yourself from the power of the past, you will find that it is completely possible.

Anxiety is experienced in the body as well as the mind. People who are alarmed by the changes in their bodies often turn to the left side of the brain to solve their dilemmas. As you probably know, brooding, worrying, and focusing on what-if scenarios only serves to keep the amygdala in a state of heightened arousal. If you recognize yourself as having neurotic tendencies, then the first step is to learn how to notice and work with anxiety in your body. Challenging expectations that are the products of splitting and old emotional memories and replacing them with realistic goals may help you out of many difficult situations. Learning to calm your emotions and your physical state of hypervigilance will provide you with the energy you need to make major changes in your life.

CHAPTER 13

Subduing Known Triggers

Prevention is the best medicine. Throughout this book I have suggested ways to learn how to recognize the triggers and emotional memories that hold the greatest power over you. I have suggested that in a moment of overreacting, it is important to divorce yourself from these forces until you have regained your emotional balance. However, once things have settled down, it is just as important to return to these issues in order to work with them in ways that diminish the power they hold over you.

The Power of Beliefs

Our minds work very quickly as we process events and sharpen our understanding of what is happening. While one part of the brain references working knowledge to help us perform simple tasks, other parts of the brain provide the information we need to generate conclusions about more complicated issues. The beliefs we draw on in these moments are accumulated from multiple experiences, many of which were acquired in childhood. Some of these beliefs incorporate positions that were held by our parents and other adults who influenced our development. Other beliefs were formed by more recent experiences, including ideas we were exposed to through books or TV.

Even though there is still much to be learned, research suggests that certain beliefs can create problems and compromise our coping mechanisms. Drs. Daniel Molden, Jason Plaks, and Carol Dweck (2006) describe two different approaches people tend to take when they form conclusions about themselves and others. *Entity thinkers* see things as fixed realities, while *incremental thinkers* look at the layers that make up the whole. Your style makes all the difference in the conclusions you reach and in many of the feelings that are consequently generated.

Entity Thinking

Entity thinkers believe that people are a certain way and that they are unlikely to change. They view the characteristics or attributes they have assigned as being absolute, and they usually have a philosophy about human nature to back up their position. For example, Jake sees his son Paul watching TV instead of doing his homework or putting his clean laundry away. In Jake's mind, Paul is the kind of person who will avoid work whenever he can and use other people to get away with it. He suspects that people are just born that way and remembers that his sister was also born lazy. His parents were always spending money on tutors for her and wasted a lot of the family's financial resources trying to get her through school. After all the work they put into helping her get accepted to a university, she ended up failing out anyway because she was too lazy to do the work. Jake's son Paul seems to be made of the same cloth.

There are many problems with this approach to reasoning. Once an entity thinker assigns a characteristic to someone, it is very difficult to alter that perception. If Jake believes that Paul is simply born that way and that any effort to help him is ultimately a waste, he will give up trying to help Paul change. Obviously, this means Paul won't get help he could probably benefit from, but it also makes Jake predisposed to come to rapid conclusions that support his viewpoint. His resentment and despair about his son's character will grow deeper, partially because he will conclude that Jake is being lazy in situations in which laziness isn't actually a factor.

Jake's approach to life as an entity thinker also applies to decisions he has made about himself. If there were things in his life he didn't instantly excel at, he probably came to global decisions about his own attributes as well. For example, when he couldn't quite get the sense of timing required to hit a baseball, he decided that he just wasn't athletic. Rather than work at getting better, he concluded that he just didn't have what it took to play baseball, or perhaps any sport, and moved on to something that came more easily. Entity thinkers are inclined to see themselves as failures and give up when they encounter small challenges. They are more inclined to see things as beyond their control and less likely to believe that change is possible. Without a goal that you believe in, this becomes a self-fulfilling prophecy.

Incremental Thinking

Incremental thinkers understand that people pass through different stages and that there are multiple factors that influence behavior in every situation. They tend to see people as being malleable or open to improvement. For example, if Jake notices that his son Paul is watching TV instead of doing his math homework, he might question what is causing his son to act this way. He might wonder if Paul is taking the lazy way through school or if he is avoiding his homework for a reason. He knows that when Paul was younger he tended to be very critical of himself and easily frustrated. He wonders if he can do anything to help his son tackle his responsibility and decides to have a talk with him. After he learns that Paul doesn't understand the math and blames his teacher for his inability to get it, Jake acknowledges that it's hard to sit down with homework that makes you feel stupid for not getting it. He offers to stay with Paul and help him look through the textbook until they find the lesson that was difficult for Paul to follow in class. Although Paul initially squirms and shows impatience, his father notices that, after a few minutes, Paul's face lights up as he sighs with huge relief. Paul gives his father a big grin and announces that he can finish the homework in ten minutes now—it's really easy. Jake feels proud of his son and at the same time sad as he remembers how his parents used to yell at his sister for being lazy and stupid. With all of those negative messages, it was no wonder that she dropped out of college.

When Jake encounters a setback in his own life, he tries to think about what needs to be improved. He acknowledges that there are some things that come to him easier than others, but he knows that practice makes all the difference. He tries to set a goal that is realistic, even if he knows he'll have to work at it before he gets it right. He also knows that he performs better under certain circumstances. Just as with his son Paul, it helps when someone is there to give him support and offer strategies to help him try a new approach. Jake is known as being goal directed and for persevering when things get tough. That style has helped him in his job, his marriage, and, just now, with his son.

Rewriting the Script

Narrative therapists Michael White and David Epston (1990) suggest that the way we tell the story determines the outcome. Often, the most painful incidents from the past have been filed away without being fully understood or questioned. Many of these unprocessed experiences form the "road map" we refer to when we need help figuring out what lies ahead on the highway we are traveling. Imagine how you would feel if someone told you that the map you are using is thirty years old and that new towns, shopping areas, and points of interest have sprung up all over the area. Wouldn't you be curious and ask for an updated map?

When we focus on past failures or the parts of ourselves we dislike, our version of the situation is automatically problem focused and saturated with negativity. Narrative therapists understand how quickly things can turn around when people are guided to remember times when they succeeded and those things that they did to achieve that preferred outcome. Therapist Michael White (1989) encouraged people to think about the ways that they fought self-defeat and how to reconnect with the parts that carried efficacy. He gently inserted alternative explanations that allowed a shift in the way the situation and the outcome might develop. When the situation and potential outcome can be revised, the old map can be replaced.

Challenging Your Expectations

What we think will happen often determines the outcome. This point was made clear to me in a karate class I observed. When the students were asked if they could split a block of wood with their hands, most of them took one look at the thick piece of wood and decided that there was no way they could break the wood without shattering their hands at the same time. A few students made a gesture of taking a swipe at the wood, but it was obvious that they were holding themselves back in self-protection. When the instructor showed them the trick of holding their fingers a certain way and demonstrated how easily the wood snaps, the students approached it quite differently. After the first student followed the instructions and succeeded, the mood in the room changed from uncertainty to eagerness. Once the students believed that they were capable and had seen others succeed, everything turned around. This time, they approached the situation with confidence and vigor and shattered the blocks of wood exactly as they expected.

As I described in chapter 5, splitting and flooding can put us in the "all bad" drawer, where we will only find memories of disappointment and defeat. When we can replace the doubt that stems from this perspective with the possibilities that can only be discovered when we have closed that drawer, then there will be new options that somehow we just hadn't noticed before.

Challenging Old Emotional Memories

Going back to painful emotional memories is hard but necessary work if we want to reduce the power of the curses in Pandora's box. Even when we have tried to write these memories off or dismiss them, they have a way of reinserting themselves when we are feeling vulnerable. In a moment of doubt or frustration, emotional memories are rekindled without our awareness. The better we know the contents of Pandora's box, the easier it will be to recognize old messages and their origins, and the better prepared we'll be to loosen their grip and figure out how to effectively shut the box.

Some of the most painful revived beliefs are about whether we are loveable or good enough. Other important memories concern the people we live and work with and our ability to trust and depend on them. We have beliefs about power, fairness, forgiveness, and competence—all driving forces that can trigger emotional overreactions.

Many of the end-of-chapter exercises were written to help you identify some of the themes that may emerge when you are vulnerable. If you are like the clients I have worked with, then your greatest vulnerabilities were probably formed when you were a child and too little to have any power over the situation. Therapy is one way to explore and challenge old beliefs, but there are things that you can do on your own behalf as well.

Making Peace with the Past

It is staggering to read the research that documents how many of us have endured painful childhoods (Dube 2001). Too many children experience or witness physical abuse and trauma and suffer from anxiety or depression as a result (Heim and Nemeroff 2001). Psychologists now suspect that even children who are relatively protected don't always get the empathy and secure connection they need to achieve their potential (D. J. Siegel 1999). Although it is normal to feel angry when we think about being deprived or abused, holding on to that anger will only reinforce the beliefs that make you suspicious and reluctant to trust others. It is far better to make peace with the past.

A Multigenerational Perspective

It is not uncommon for my social work students to declare that although they feel gratified working with children who have been abused, they are filled with horror and disgust at the adult perpetrators. They think that the adults who harmed children or allowed children to be hurt are monsters who don't deserve any sympathy. They see how injured the children are as evidenced by inappropriate behaviors like lying, stealing, hurting themselves, and even abusing other children. I ask my class to fast-forward and predict what their young clients might be like in twenty years if treatment fails. I then ask them to rewind the years and imagine that they are working with their clients' parents when these people were teenagers. I ask them to see these clients as they were when they were young and to imagine the families and circumstances they grew up with. This exercise is all it takes for students to realize that trauma is most often multigenerational. It is easy to love the victim and blame the aggressor, but it is confusing when the aggressor is also viewed as victim.

I have found that, most of the time, my clients are people who are doing the best they can with what they have. Often, pain begets pain, and people end up repeating what was done to them. It is impossible to forgive someone when we view their behavior as purposeful, but quite possible when we begin to take into consideration the challenges, limitations, and burdens that may have prevented them from doing things differently.

Harmful Family Myths

Dr. Froma Walsh (1988) once told me that her most useful training came from her undergraduate courses in anthropology. Learning to search for and respect the details that make cultures unique taught her a valuable lesson in how to understand the values and beliefs that operate in every family she works with. Even when family members share the same ethnic, religious, and educational backgrounds, there are profound differences in how each member of a family conducts her life.

The way we want things done is often informed by family rules and customs we have adopted without question. For example, families tend to serve certain foods on the holidays and to uphold a moral code regarding what is appropriate and unacceptable behavior. Family therapists know that families have their own values, customs, and informal rules about displays of affection, privacy, dependency, gender-based competency, and family obligations. These become assumed truths that are easily absorbed and seldom challenged. Often, examining these things from a historical perspective is the first step of the change process.

■ ANN'S STORY

Dr. Ann Hartman illustrated this point by telling a story from her own family (Hartman 1988). She noticed that the adults on her mother's side of the family were uncomfortable with physical affection, even though they all seemed to have a great deal of love for each other. They were particularly standoffish toward the children, giving them polite nods instead of hugs and kisses. Puzzled by her own sharp instinct to keep a distance from the children she adored, she decided to search for family stories that might shed light on the situation.

The eldest living relative on her mother's side of the family did not seem at all puzzled by this family pattern. She told Ann that shortly after the family immigrated to the United States, there was an outbreak of tuberculosis. She recalled how distraught the family was when her young niece was diagnosed with it and instructed to go to an upstate sanitarium. Just the week before, they had all been enjoying a birthday party celebration for her four-year-old son. Everyone had seemed so happy. Tears fell down her cheeks as she recalled the scene at the train station: her niece scooping her two small children into her embrace as she promised that Mommy would get stronger and come back to them. In those days, very few returned alive. The family said good-bye to this beautiful young mother and prepared themselves for the worst. A year later, their niece did return—fully rested and healed. But the first thing she did was visit the graves of her two children, who had died months before from tuberculosis. From that day on, it was silently forbidden to kiss a child for fear that it would be a kiss that would consign a child to death.

Making peace with the past often requires us to stop thinking in terms of fault and instead accept that there is usually a context and background involved in events that end badly. Rethinking the context is not the same as denying that a bad thing has happened, but it may allow you to replace anger and resentment with a sad recognition of shared disappointments and hardships. Instead of focusing on how difficult it was for her to be affectionate with children or being resentful that affection was withheld from her when she was young, Ann could feel compassion for herself and all the generations that had struggled with unresolved loss.

Removing the Burden of Shame or Personal Failure

Making peace with the past also requires us to deal with our own stored memories of personal failure. Often the shame and anger we hold on to are based entirely on conclusions that were formed through the lens of childhood. Children frequently get caught up in issues that more appropriately belong to their parents. For example, it is not uncommon for a mother who despises a particular quality in her partner to rage at her son when he does something that suggests the same trait. The boy might feel confused and perhaps unfairly attacked but will also absorb a full dose of shame. While an adult might challenge the attack or even blow it off, a child would probably believe that his mother is right, even if she is being unfair. Because children need to preserve a loving bond with their parents, it would be easier for him to swallow the resentment and take the anger out on himself.

Although the shame and anger can remain buried for a long time, these feelings can be revived in full force when a similar situation evokes that emotional memory. Should that occur, a childlike state of helplessness, resentment, and despair will quickly follow.

On bad days, we might simply allow verdicts that sealed a sense of failure to stand uncontested, but on a day that we are ready to challenge the past, we can choose to fight. One strategy involves revisiting childhood pain from an adult perspective. Rather than accepting the judgments that have been passed down, you can empower your child-self to reexamine the situation. In many ways, this is like announcing a new trial to contest old verdicts. If you are empowered to challenge conclusions about yourself and others that have wounded you deeply, you may arrive at a new understanding. Perhaps there is circumstantial evidence that can be brought to a new trial, particularly now that, as an adult, you can comprehend how children are often used as scapegoats and put in the middle of their parents' conflicts.

Each of us has good reason to revisit old memories when we have the option of challenging the verdicts that were handed out to us. When we do that, we may realize how much agony was created over such minor transgressions. Even if you conclude that you really did deserve some of the blame that you have been saddled with, don't you think you've served enough time?

Using the Future to Shape the Present

When people I work with become overly pessimistic because of difficulties or deprivations they suffered in childhood, I tell them about the power of the future. Dr. Luigi Boscolo (1993) suggested that the pull toward the future can be as powerful as the pull toward the past if we can only learn how to harness its power. Let's say you can't decide whether or not to spend some of your savings to purchase a wingback chair that just went on sale. If you turn toward the past to guide you, you might think about the times you walked away from similar bargains and never found a comparable item at the price you decided to pass on. You could start to chastise yourself for letting good opportunities go by and hate your tendency to take so long to make every decision. As the memory drawer of other times you failed to act promptly swings open, old emotional memories of things that you let pass you by add to your emotional experience. The anxiety and self-doubt could cripple you.

But if you were able to look into the future in this fantasy example, you might see that in three months you would receive an amazing job opportunity. This wonderful new position would require that you spend three months in Paris to get some additional training and then three months at the company's headquarters in Hawaii. When you return from your training, you'd have the opportunity to move into a new home with an easy commute to your job. Your home would be a more modern space, and the large pieces of furniture you've tended to like in the past wouldn't really fit in. With that vision of the future in mind, do you think that the decision about purchasing a new chair would still be difficult?

There are no crystal balls to tell us our future, but clearly thought-out goals can be just as powerful. It is understandable to think about the parts of yourself that have been stifled because of your past, but instead of focusing on the past, use that information to create awareness of who you would like to become under different circumstances. It is helpful to notice that the present is better than the past, but look ahead. The tactics you used to get this far in life are only part of the recipe that defines you. Dr. Susan Harter (Harter et al. 1997) has noted that we all have multiple selves that are capable of emerging under the right circumstances. Earlier situations and responsibilities may have confined us to use only those parts of ourselves that were needed at certain points in our lives. After living in this way for a number of years, we may forget that there are other parts of us that are on the back burner. Just as a plant needs warmth and sunlight to prepare to flower, the parts of yourself that you want to reconnect with might benefit from a wake-up call that the time to move forward has arrived.

Describe to yourself the person you would like to be in the next ten years of your life. If you can describe those qualities, then you have a powerful vision to guide you. You can't always control the world around you, but aspiring to become that person can connect you to the possibility of change and the power to achieve it that all adults possess.

Conclusion

The Decade of the Brain led to new insights that help us understand human suffering as well as resilience. This should be welcome news to people who have struggled with abrupt episodes of anger, anguish, and distress with no idea of why it happens or how to stop it.

Learning to stop overreacting requires patience and persistence. Mind and body, present and past are all parts of the puzzle that make up an emotional overreaction. It is my hope that you will be able to use the information in this book to find a new way to put these pieces together so that the picture you create is the best one possible for you and the people you love.

Reading Recommendations

Books

Brown, B. 2007. *I Thought It Was Just Me (But It Isn't): Telling the Truth About Perfectionism, Inadequacy, and Power.* New York: Penguin Books/Gotham.

Hanson, R., and R. Mendius. 2009. *Buddha's Brain: The Practical Neuroscience of Happiness, Love, and Wisdom.* Oakland, CA: New Harbinger.

Johnson, S. 2008. *Hold Me Tight: Seven Conversations for a Lifetime of Love.* New York: Little Brown.

Siegel, D. J., and M. Hartzell. 2003. *Parenting from the Inside Out: How a Deeper Self-Understanding Can Help You Raise Children Who Thrive.* New York: Penguin.

Siegel, J. P. 2000. *What Children Learn from Their Parents' Marriage.* New York: Harper Collins.

Williams, M., J. Teasdale, Z. Segal, and J. Kabat-Zinn. 2007. *The Mindful Way through Depression: Freeing Yourself from Chronic Unhappiness.* New York: Guilford Press.

Workbooks

Jacobs, B. 2004. *Writing for Emotional Balance: A Guided Journal to Help You Manage Overwhelming Emotions.* Oakland, CA: New Harbinger.

Spradlin, S. E. 2003. *Don't Let Your Emotions Run Your Life: How Dialectical Behavior Therapy Can Put You in Control.* Oakland, CA: New Harbinger.

References

Augustine, A., and S. H. Hemenover. 2009. On the relative effective-
ness of affect regulation strategies: A meta-analysis. *Cognition and
Emotion* 23:1181–1220.

Baer, R. A., and D. B. Huss. 2008. Mindfulness- and acceptance-
based therapy. In *Twenty-First Century Psychotherapies*, edited by Jay
LeBow. Hoboken, NJ: John Wiley.

Bandura, A. 1997. *Self-Efficacy: The Exercise of Control*. New York:
Freeman.

Beck, A. 1976. *Cognitive Therapy and the Emotional Disorders*. Madison,
CT: International Universities Press.

Benjamin, L. S., and F. J. Friedrich. 1991. Contributions of structural
analysis of social behavior (SASB) to the bridge between cognitive science and a science of object relations. In *Person, Schemas
and Maladaptive Interpersonal Patterns*, edited by M. J. Horowitz.
Chicago: University of Chicago Press.

Benjamin, L. S., J. Rothweiler, J. Conrad, and K. L. Critchfield. 2006.
The use of structural analysis of social behavior (SASB) as an assessment tool. *Annual Review of Clinical Psychology* 2:83–109.

Boscolo, L. 1993. *The Times of Time*. New York: Norton.

Brown, B. 2006. Shame resilience theory: A grounded theory of women and shame. *Families in Society* 87:43–52.

Bushman, B. J. 2002. Does venting anger feed or extinguish the flame? *Personality and Social Psychology Bulletin* 28:724–731.

Cicchetti, D., and D. Tucker. 1994. Development and self-regulatory structures of the mind. *Development and Psychopathology* 6:533–549.

Coleman, D. 1998. *Working with Emotional Intelligence*. New York: Bantam.

Compton, R. J. 2003. The interface between emotion and attention. *Behavioral and Cognitive Neuroscience Review* 2:115–129.

Cozolino, L. J. 2002. *The Neuroscience of Psychotherapy: Building and Rebuilding the Human Brain*. New York: Norton.

Crockett, M. J. 2009. The neurochemistry of fairness: Clarifying the link between serotonin and prosocial behavior. *Annals of the New York Academy of Sciences* 1167:76–86.

Cyders, M. A., and G. T. Smith. 2007. Mood-based rash action and its components: Positive and negative urgency. *Personality and Individual Differences* 43:839–850.

———. 2008. Emotion-based dispositions to rash action: Positive and negative urgency. *Psychological Bulletin* 134:807–828.

Depue, R. A., and P. F. Collins. 1999. Neurobiology of the structure of personality: Facilitation of incentive motivation and extraversion. *Behavioral and Brain Sciences* 22:491–517.

DeZulueta, F. 2006. The treatment of psychological trauma from the perspective of attachment research. *Journal of Family Therapy* 28:334–351.

Dube, S. R., R. F. Anda, V. J. Felitti, D. P. Chapman, D. F. Williamson, and W. H. Giles. 2001. Childhood abuse, household dysfunction and the risk of attempted suicide throughout the life span: Findings from the Adverse Childhood Experiences Study. *Journal of the American Medical Association* 286(24):3089-3096.

Eisenberger, N., and M. D. Lieberman. 2004. Why rejection hurts: A common neural alarm system for physical and social pain. *Trends in Cognitive Science* 8:294–300.

Erikson, E. 1950. *Childhood and Society*. New York: Norton.

Farmer, R. L. 2009. *Neuroscience and Social Work Practice: The Missing Link*. Newbury Park, CA: Sage.

Fishbane, M. D. 2007. Wired to connect: Neuroscience, relationships, and therapy. *Family Process* 46:395–412.

Fosha, D. 2000. *The Transforming Power of Affect: A Model for Accelerated Change*. New York: Basic Books.

Gohm, C. L. 2003. Mood regulation and emotional intelligence. *Journal of Personality and Social Psychology* 84:594–607.

Goldin, P. R., T. Manber-Ball, K. Werner, R. Heimberg, and J. J. Gross. 2009. Neural mechanisms of cognitive reappraisal of negative self-beliefs in social anxiety disorder. *Biological Psychiatry* 66:1091–1099.

Gottman, J. M. 1998. Psychology and the study of marital processes. *Annual Review of Psychology* 49:169–197.

Grawe, K. 2006. *Neuropsychotherapy: How the Neurosciences Inform Effective Psychotherapy*. Mahwah, NJ: Lawrence Erlbaum.

Haas, B. W., K. Omura, R. T. Constable, and T. Canli. 2007. Emotional conflict and neuroticism: Personality and activation of the amygdala. *Behavioral Neuroscience* 121:249–256.

Hanson, R., and R. Mendius. 2009. *Buddha's Brain. The Practical Neuroscience of Happiness, Love, and Wisdom*. Oakland, CA: New Harbinger.

Harter, S., S. Bresneck, H. A. Bouchey, and N. R. Whitesell. 1997. The development of multiple role-related selves during adolescence. *Development and Psychopathology* 9:835–854.

Hartman, A. 1988. Personal communication.

Hedwig, T., and S. Epstein. 1998. Temperament and personality theory: The perspective of cognitive-experiential self theory. *School Psychology Review* 27:534–550.

Heim, C., and C. B. Nemeroff. 2001. The role of childhood trauma in the neurobiology of mood and anxiety disorders: Preclinical and clinical studies. *Biological Psychiatry* 49:1023–1039.

Hirsh, J. B., and M. Inzlicht. 2008. The devil you know: Neuroticism predicts neural response to uncertainty. *Psychological Science* 19: 962–967.

Hoobler, J. M., and D. J. Brass. 2006. Abusive supervision and family undermining as displaced aggression. *Journal of Applied Psychology* 91:1125–1133.

Horowitz, M. J. 1991. Person schemas. In *Schemas and Maladaptive Interpersonal Patterns*, edited by Mardi J. Horowitz. Chicago: University of Chicago Press.

Jacobs, B. 2004. *Writing for Emotional Balance: A Guided Journal to Help You Manage Overwhelming Emotions*. Oakland, CA: New Harbinger.

Judge, T. A., J. A. LePine, and B. L. Rich. 2006. Loving yourself abundantly: Relationship of the narcissistic personality to self- and other perceptions of workplace deviance, leadership, and task and contextual performance. *Journal of Applied Psychology* 91:762–776.

Kandel, E. R. 1998. A new intellectual framework for psychiatry. *American Journal of Psychiatry* 155:457–469.

———. 1999. Biology and the future of psychoanalysis: A new intellectual framework for psychiatry revisited. *American Journal of Psychiatry* 156:505–524.

Krystal, H. 1988. *Integration and Self-Healing: Affect, Trauma, Alexithymia*. Hillsdale, NJ: The Analytic Press.

LaBar, K. S., and R. Cabeza. 2006. Cognitive neuroscience of emotional memory. *Nature Reviews* 7:54–64.

Leary, M. R., J. Twenge, and E. Quinlivan. 2006. Interpersonal rejection as a determinant of anger and aggression. *Personality and Social Psychology Review* 10:111–132.

Lewis, M. D. 2005a. Bridging emotion theory and neurobiology through dynamic systems modeling. *Behavioral and Brain Sciences* 28:169–193.

———. 2005b. An emerging dialogue among social scientists and neuroscientists on the causal bases of emotion. *Behavioral and Brain Sciences* 28:223–245.

Lewis, M. D., and R. Todd. 2007. The self-regulating brain: Cortical and subcortical feedback and the development of intelligent action. *Cognitive Development* 22:406–450.

Lieberman, M. D., N. I. Eisenberger, M. J. Crockett, S. M. Tom, and J. Pfeifer. 2007. Putting feelings into words: Affect labeling disrupts amygdala activity in response to affective stimuli. *Psychological Science* 18:421–428.

Meissner, W. W. 1980. The problem of internalization and structure formation. *International Journal of Psychoanalysis* 61:237–247.

———. 1986. The earliest internalizations. In *Self and Object Constancy*, edited by R. Lax and S. Bach. New York: Guilford Press.

Molden, D. C., J. E. Plaks, and C. S. Dweck. 2006. Meaningful social inferences: Effects of implicit theories on inferential processes. *Journal of Experimental Social Psychology* 42:738–752.

Moses, E. B. T., and D. H. Barlow. 2006. A new unified treatment approach for emotional disorders based on emotion science. *Current Directions in Psychological Science* 15:146–150.

Ochsner, K. N., and J. J. Gross. 2007. The neural architecture of emotion regulation. In *Handbook of Emotion Regulation*, edited by J. J. Gross. New York: Guilford Press.

Penhaligon, N. L., W. Louis, and S. L. Restubog. 2009. Emotional anguish at work: The mediating role of perceived rejection on work-group mistreatment and affective outcomes. *Journal of Occupational Health Psychology* 14:34–45.

Penney, L. J., and P. E. Spector. 2002. Narcissism and counterproductive work behavior: Do bigger egos mean bigger problems? *International Journal of Selection and Assessment* 10:126–134.

Phelps, J. E., and E. A. LeDoux. 2005. Contributions of the amygdala to emotion processing: From animal models to human behavior. *Neuron* 48:175–187.

Rauch, S., L. Shin, and C. Wright. 2003. Neuroimaging studies of amygdala function in anxiety disorders. *Annals of the New York Society of Science* 985:389–410.

Ray, R. D., K. N. Ochsner, J. C. Cooper, E. R. Robertson, J. D. E. Gabrieli, and J. J. Gross. 2005. Individual differences in trait rumination and the neural systems supporting cognitive reappraisal. *Cognitive, Affective, and Behavioral Neuroscience* 5:156–168.

Rhodewalt, F., and C. C. Morf. 1998. On self-aggrandizement and anger: A temporal analysis of narcissism and affective reactions to success and failure. *Journal of Personality and Social Psychology* 74:672–685.

Schore, A. N. 2002. *Affect Dysregulation and Disorders of the Self.* New York: Norton.

———. 2003a. *Affect Regulation and the Repair of the Self.* New York: Norton.

———. 2003b. Early relational trauma, disorganized attachment, and the development of a predisposition to violence. In *Healing Trauma: Attachment, Mind, Body and Brain*, edited by Marion F. Solomon and Daniel J. Siegel. New York: Norton.

Schore, J. R., and A. N. Schore. 2008. Modern attachment theory: The central role of affect regulation in development and treatment. *Clinical Social Work Journal* 36:9–20.

Seligman, M. E. 1975. *Helplessness: On Depression, Development and Death.* San Francisco: Freeman.

Siegel, D. J. 1999. *The Developing Mind.* New York: Guilford Press.

———. 2003. An interpersonal neurobiology of psychotherapy: The developing mind and the resolution of trauma. In *Healing Trauma:*

Attachment, Mind, Body and Brain, edited by Marion Solomon and D. J. Siegel. New York: Norton.

Siegel, D. J., and M. Hartzell. 2003. *Parenting from the Inside Out: How a Deeper Self-Understanding Can Help You Raise Children Who Thrive*. New York: Penguin.

Siegel, J. P. 1992. *Repairing Intimacy: An Object Relations Approach to Couples Therapy*. Northvale, NJ: Jason Aronson.

————. 2000. *What Children Learn from Their Parents' Marriage*. New York: Harper Collins.

————. 2004. Identification as a focal point in couple therapy. *Psychoanalytic Inquiry* 24:406–419.

————. 2006. Dyadic splitting in partner relational disorders. *Journal of Family Psychology* 20:418–422.

Smith, R. H., and S. H. Kim. 2007. Comprehending envy. *Psychological Bulletin* 133:46–64.

Stucke T., and S. Sporer. 2002. Who's to blame? Narcissism and self-serving attributions following feedback. *European Journal of Personality* 17:465–478.

Suls, J., and R. Martin. 2005. The daily life of the garden-variety neurotic: Reactivity, stressor exposure, mood spillover, and maladaptive coping. *Journal of Personality* 73:1485–1510.

Van der Kolk, B. A., A. C. McFarlane, and L. Weisaeth, eds. 1996. *Traumatic Stress: The Effects of Overwhelming Experience on Mind, Body, and Society*. New York: Guilford Press.

Vecchio, R. P. 2000. Negative emotion in the workplace: Employee jealousy and envy. *International Journal of Stress Management* 7:161–179.

————. 2005. Explorations in employee envy: Feeling envious and feeling envied. *Cognition and Emotion* 19:69–81.

Viamontes, G. I., and B. C. Beitman. 2006. Neural substrates of psychotherapeutic change: Part 1 and part 11. *Psychiatric Annals* 36:225–247.

Walker, M. P., and E. van der Helm. 2009. Overnight therapy? The role of sleep in emotional brain processing. *Psychology Bulletin* 135:731–748.

Walsh, F. 1988. Personal communication.

White, M. 1989. *Selected Papers.* Adelaide, Australia: Dulwich Centre Publications.

White, M., and D. Epston. 1990. *Narrative Means to Therapeutic Ends.* New York: Norton.

Williams, J. M., and J. Teasdale. 2007. *The Mindful Way Through Depression: Freeing Yourself from Chronic Unhappiness.* New York: Guilford Press.

Young, J. E., J. Klosko, and M. Weishaar. 2003. *Schema Therapy.* New York: Guilford Press.

Judith P. Siegel, Ph.D., LCSW, is associate professor at Silver School of Social Work at New York University. She has published extensively in the field of family therapy and has presented throughout the United States. She has also appeared on *The Today Show* and *Good Morning America*.